AMERICAN
FOLK ART
QUILTS

AMERICAN
FOLK ART
QUILTS

MAGGI MCCORMICK GORDON

TRAFALGAR SQUARE BOOKS

North Pomfret, Vermont

First published in the United States of America
in 2007 by Trafalgar Square Books
North Pomfret, Vermont 05053

Editor: Marie Clayton
Designer: Sue Rose
Photographer: Mark Hines

Printed in Taiwan

Library of Congress Control Number: 2007927438

ISBN: 978-1-57076-400-4

CONTENTS

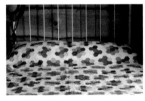

INTRODUCTION

OCTAGON
1870–1890

Also called
Honeycomb, or
Snowball, or Job's
Troubles, this quilt
pattern uses octagon
linked by small
squares. This example
is a "charm" quilt in
which none of the
fabrics used to make
the octagons is
repeated. Made by
Maria Mitchell Brown
Allen, born in 1832 in
Rio, Wisconsin, it dates
from about 1870–1890.
Maria and her husband
Seth Allen (1824–1906)
had twelve children, so
quilts would have been
needed in quantity.

Maker Maria Mitchell
Brown Allen (1832–?)
76 x 68 in.
(193 x 173 cm)

ID 1973.127.1

THE TERM "FOLK ART" encompasses many ideas and theories. With quilts, it is often used to describe naive examples by quilters with no training in art or design. It may refer to quilts made by a child or beginner, full of charming mistakes, anomalies of scale or unusual color combinations. We have chosen quilts to represent the exuberant output from American quiltmakers over the past 175 years. Some are beautifully designed and stitched by unknown masters; others are folk art at its most basic.

Much of the work immediately identified as "folk art" interprets forms from nature, so Floral Quilts has examples of recognizable or stylized flowers and related objects. Wholecloth Quilts shows the variety within a group of similarly constructed quilts. All are made from fabric that appears to be a single piece (though may be several pieces joined together), quilted to create beautifully textured bedcovers. Embellished Quilts are decorated in some way, and are fascinating examples of the creativity of the folk artist. Embroidery is the method most often used, and the examples in this chapter offer different ways to use decorative stitching to enhance a piece.

Signature Quilts are a diverse group of examples; signatures are the only thing they have in common. Signing blocks that were then incorporated into a quilt top was a way of honoring a person or family leaving, perhaps to journey westward. Other signature quilts, in which participants paid to have their names included, were made as fundraisers for a civic or religious institution and were sometimes auctioned off to raise additional money or presented to a worthy personage as a mark of respect. These quilts could be pieced or appliquéd, and the chapter contains examples of both. Geometric Quilts includes bedcovers and quilt tops based on geometric shapes combined to create repeating patterns made lively with color combinations and interesting in their interpretation of traditional designs. Small Quilts includes both crib quilts and doll quilts—most examples were subjected to much love and laundering, but our selection shows the diversity that can be found among these little treasures.

The Workbook chapter contains information on basic techniques and step-by-step instructions for making six quilts, one from each chapter. Templates for the projects are included, and the techniques used to make the other quilts in the book are outlined. Terms that relate to the quilts and techniques in the book are listed in the Glossary.

All the quilts in this book are part of the wonderful collection of the Wisconsin Historical Society, based in Madison, Wisconsin (see page 140). Without the support and enthusiasm of its staff the book could not have happened, and I thank them for all the time and energy they devoted to making sure it did. Choosing was a difficult task, and I hope readers will enjoy the final selection.

QUILTMAKING AND FOLK ART

FOLK ARTISTS work in many media and in every culture around the globe. By some definitions, quilters are all folk artists, working with everyday materials to fashion a useful creation. The craft-versus-art argument continues to present an academic dilemma for historians and curators, and those curating or studying quilts are no exception.

Art quilts nonwithstanding, quilting has long been considered a craft, a way of making household objects that have everyday uses. Most quilts made before the late twentieth century, when the art quilt movement began and became widespread, were made to be used. They were a way of keeping warm in cold weather, very necessary before the advent of central heating. That many of them were also beautiful enough to be used to decorate the bed is a tribute to the myriad makers whose pride in their work and innate, but generally untrained, creative instincts gave them the ability to turn out quilts that they were happy to have on display.

Early Quilting

Quilts were not always made to go onto beds. Early quilted items were more often than not garments, from the vests wore by medieval archer-soldiers to pad their protective chain-mail armor to the exquisitely worked waistcoats, petticoats, and baby bonnets of wealthy European aristocrats of the seventeenth century. In fact, ladies' petticoats became so elaborate that skirts were hiked up deliberately and permanently to show off the undergarment beneath.

Quilted hangings were used to enclose beds to ward off drafts and to provide some privacy in the cold stone castles and manor houses occupied by huge numbers of people from the end of the Middle Ages, and began to find their way onto the bed itself by the seventeenth and eighteenth centuries. By the beginning of the nineteenth century, the use of the quilt as a bedcover was widespread, and untold numbers were made, especially in Britain and North America. Quilts were also made in the Scandinavian countries and the German areas, and somewhat surprisingly in the south of France, where they are very thick and known as "boutis," but the English-speaking world was the main locus of the craft. While an urban myth exists expounding the theory that the pattern generally known as Cathedral Window was called Mayflower in North America because the travelers on that vessel made examples during the

WISCONSIN IDEA SAMPLER QUILT 1978–1979

Each patchwork block in this green, blue, red, white, and brown quilt is a different pattern, which has been chosen for its significance to the history and culture of Wisconsin; for example, the Churn Dash block (upper left) represents the dairy industry, a mainstay of the state's agricultural heritage and economy. The quilt was made in the fall of 1978 by Kathleen L. Briggs of Milwaukee for the Wisconsin Arts Board and the State of Wisconsin as a pilot project to commemorate quilting's past in the state and to stimulate its revival.

Maker   Kathleen L. Briggs (b. 1938)
88 x 88 in.
(224 x 224 cm)

ID 1979.37

BENNINGTON FLAG
1976

Made as a Bicentennial tribute in 1976, this red, white, and blue Bennington-style flag has an arch of eleven white stars over a large "76" with a star in each top corner of the blue field in the left top corner.   Each star has seven points. The quilt is signed by 157 people and marked "Lakeview Seniors/1776–1796."   Lakeview is thought to refer to the Lakeview Manor Retirement Home in Madison, Wisconsin.

Makers Members of Lakeview Community
88 x 62 in.
(224 x 157 cm)

ID 1976.239

journey, it is unlikely. The folded technique would not have lent itself to being worked on a rolling ship, and there were few women aboard. But as more and more people settled in the colonies along the Atlantic coast, quilts and quilt patterns were transported back and forth between the British homeland and North America. Families brought their household effects with them to start new lives along the eastern seaboard, and quilts were often among those belongings. The cold winters, especially in New England and Canada, led colonists to make quilts, using whatever scraps were at hand, since fabric was scarce and expensive. At times, the British government outlawed both spinning wheels and looms in the colonies as a way to protect the thriving and lucrative textile industry based mainly in Liverpool and Manchester on the west coast of England, so virtually all the fabric available to the colonial quiltmakers was either imported at huge expense or recycled from dressmaking, old clothes, or worn household linens. Of course, few colonial-era quilts have survived, but by the early 1800s after independence, cloth had become easier to obtain and was usually produced locally in the burgeoning textile mills that were springing up all over New England.

American Quilts

As the young United States continued to attract immigrants to freedom and the promise of a better life, quilts continued to arrive in North America and quilt patterns continued being passed from one maker to another on both sides of the Atlantic. Since most of the early settlers were from Britain, colonial and then federal quiltmaking was influenced by the traditions from several parts of the British Isles. Wholecloth quilts, widespread in the northeast of England and parts of Wales, are among the earliest American examples. Traditional Welsh quiltmaking, with its use of somber plain colors and wool fabrics cut in fairly large units, certainly influenced the design of many early Amish quilts, and the patchwork blocks that appear in the borders of English medallion-style quilts turn up as fully fledged block patterns in American quilts as the nineteenth century moved the country toward the Civil War. Quilts were a valuable commodity during that conflict

This unique quilt has thirty-six blocks, each decorated with a necktie. The ties are created from real ones belonging to members of the Milwaukee Metropolitan Baptist Church. Each block bears the name of the owner of the tie, all from the congregation of which the maker, Allie Crumble, an African-American born in Mississippi in about 1911, was a long-time member. After she and her husband moved to Milwaukee in 1944, she taught quilting to church seniors there—while raising ten children—and became a prolific quiltmaker.

Maker Allie Crumble
(b. 1911?)
87 x 72 in.
(221 x 183 cm)

ID 1996.118.16

with fabric again becoming a scarce resource, and many were made to raise money for the troops on both sides of the Mason-Dixon line. Both before and after the war, slaves and then freed African Americans made quilts. Many of the existing examples were made from European-style patterns to be used by the slave owners' families, but others made for their own use recall African traditions of fabric construction and design.

After the war, the last quarter of the nineteenth century became a heyday for quilts and quiltmakers. Fabric was widely available at reasonable prices, and quilts were a way for women to display some creativity in their daily lives while fulfilling their traditional domestic role. Quilts became a focus in social life, with quilting bees in rural and urban settings, and were important items for fundraising for various good causes. Crazy quilts and appliqué quilts allowed talented stitchers to show off their skills, and block patchwork became identified, if not quite correctly, as being American in origin. Throughout the early twentieth century, quilts continued to be made, especially during the Great Depression that swept the country through the 1930s, in which the make-do-and-mend aspect of making quilts became an overriding factor for many.

World War II erupted, however, and quiltmaking took a back seat as women poured into the workplace in unprecedented numbers to fill the jobs of men who had gone to the front. Postwar prosperity and a wider life outside the home meant that people bought bedcovers instead of making them, and by the 1960s many of the traditional skills had been lost. For a while, it looked as though they might be gone forever, but thanks to a dedicated band of quilters and the 1976 Bicentennial celebrations, the importance of the art and techniques of quiltmaking were recognized. A nationwide project to make celebratory quilts was launched. Books were written, classes and workshops were taught, new techniques and equipment were developed, and quiltmaking was saved for a new generation to enjoy and pass down to the next. Hopefully, quiltmaking is here to stay, whether its practitioners considered themselves folk artists or art quilters or simply makers of quilts.

THE
QUILTS

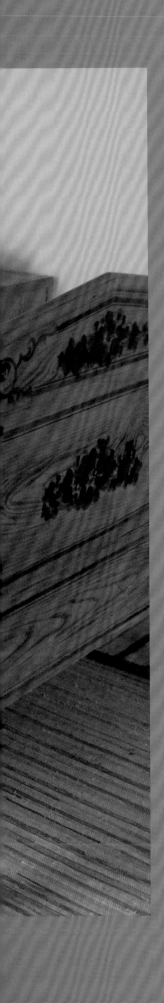

FLORAL QUILTS

The patterns that reflect the natural world, especially plants, are probably the most instantly recognized as "folk art" in quilts. Trees and flowers are used in abundance in quiltmaking, from brightly colored block appliqué quilts from the nineteenth century, including the finely wrought Baltimore album quilts made around 1850, to the delicate pastel-hued kit quilts of the 1920s, '30s, and '40s, and many traditional basket designs have "floral" names, such as the Basket of Flowers in this chapter.

THE STORY OF FLORAL QUILTS

DETAIL

President's Wreath
block, page 28. Quite
often flowers and
leaves are naturalistic
with simplified shapes.
Appliqué: red and
green on white.

ID 2005.17.1

FLOWERS, TREES, and other plants, as well as
a wide variety of animals and birds, make
up the natural world, and these have all been
favorite subjects for artists of all disciplines. A great
number of the finest quilts known are
representations of nature—some highly realistic,
others wonderfully stylized. Many of the designs
that appear on quilts falling into the category of
"folk art" are naturalistic, with simplified shapes,
while other types are more clearly based on
botanical drawings that are a representative
likeness of the original form. Folk art quilts often
have a charming naivety, but many also show a
very sophisticated workmanship and awareness
of design.

Designs and colors

Floral quilts of the nineteenth century were
predominantly appliquéd, with repeated blocks
joined edge to edge, or separated with sashing
strips, or set on point and divided by spacer
blocks. The designs were widely copied or
adapted, and all of the blocks that are now
considered traditional have myriad variations.
There are dozens of flower types found in these
patterns, some recognizable, others rather less so.
In addition to roses and carnations, there are cacti
and daisies, tulips and lilies, poppies and pansies.
Leaves take many shapes, from long and pointed
to frilled to triangulate. Vines, stems, and garlands
weave in and out, creating wreaths and sashing

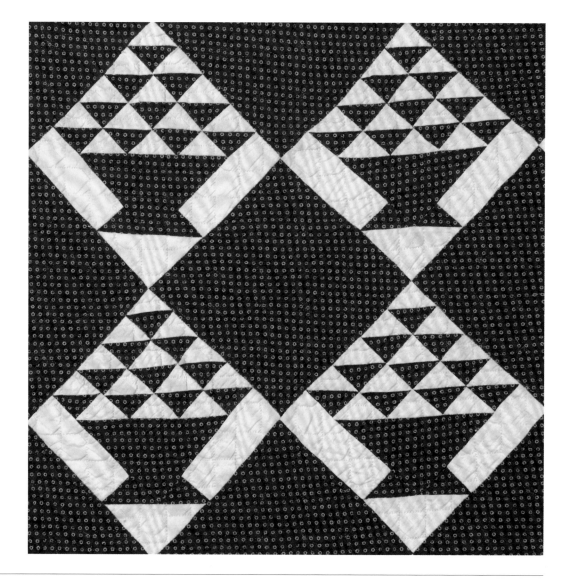

DETAIL

Basket of Flowers,
page 22. Identical
blocks may be
repeated to make up
a larger quilt.
Pieced: blue and
cream microprints.

ID 1971.183.3

and borders. Trees, especially cherry trees complete with tiny red berries, occur often, and birds and butterflies are particularly fond of insinuating themselves in among the branches. Pomegranates and pineapples appear, too, as well as strawberries and citrus fruits.

Translating forms from the outdoors into quilt patterns was a natural progression. Most women in nineteenth-century North America were firmly anchored to the land and the natural world. Their own gardens provided most of the fresh produce that appeared on the family table, especially in the rural farming areas that made up most of the vast landscape. In the burgeoning cities, most middle- and upper-class homes still had a garden, and the lady of the house was generally responsible for making sure that seeds were planted, crops tended, and bounty harvested—even if she didn't do the actual digging, hoeing, weeding, and picking herself. Her knowledge of the plants—their shapes and colors as well as their uses—was generally broad, and many of these garden experts were also quiltmakers. Bringing the outdoors inside would have been logical and normal, and no doubt many quiltmakers enjoyed having something of the outside world indoors with them through the

long, dark, cold winter months as they sat stitching by the warm fire.

The fabric colors used in floral quilts of the 1800s tended to be bright and primary: red, green, and yellow or an orange known as cheddar—usually on a cream or white background—are most widely found. Red was particularly popular with nineteenth-century quiltmakers, mainly because of a dye called Turkey red. Based on a closely guarded secret formula developed in the Middle East, Turkey red was made from madder. It was a particularly bright hue that was, more importantly, colorfast, and European chemists spent much of the eighteenth century trying to discover the secret of making it. By the mid-1800s, they had succeeded and colorfast red fabric became more widely available and affordable. Many of the most striking quilts of the latter half of the nineteenth century are simple two-color designs in red and white, but most of the floral examples contain other hues as well.

Palampores

One of the influences on quilt design in early American times was the palampore, a bedcover that was either painted or printed on cotton fabric. Originating in India in the 1600s,

DETAIL

Trees and Flowers, page 24. Flowers, birds, and butterflies, as well as different fruits, are often included. Appliqué: green, red, yellow, and brown on white.

ID 1988.188

palampores were exported to Europe, especially the British Isles where they became extremely popular, and from there to the American colonies. The original designs came from Persia and often contained a leafy tree in the center. Birds and other animals sometimes occupy the branches or the area around the trunk of the tree. The main motif became known as the Tree of Life, and its design was later incorporated into printed chintz fabrics. Both palampores and chintz were expensive and relatively rare, and individual motifs were often cut out and stitched to a less costly background fabric in a technique known as broderie persé, or Persian embroidery. Over time, the forms became more and more stylized, and developed into many of the traditional patterns we recognize today.

Baltimore album quilts

Among the most beautiful of floral quilts are the group known as Baltimore album quilts, made during the 1840s and '50s in and around Baltimore, Maryland. Their consistency of style makes them instantly recognizable. Individual blocks are appliquéd in pictorial designs, both realistic and stylized, and many of the blocks used are floral.

Patchwork and appliqué

As the making of quilts reached a zenith in the Victorian era, floral designs continued to be popular. Patchwork patterns were widely worked, including many striking baskets, the pieced buds and flowers such as Carolina Lily and Rosebud, and dozens of variations of leaves from maple to sweet gum, as well as trees made from triangles.

Appliqué, less popular than patchwork, caught the public's imagination again in the years between World Wars I and II, often in the form of kit quilts based on patterns devised by known and unknown designers and published in newspapers and magazines across the United States. Almost all of the patterns were floral, made usually in solid-colored fabrics and often in a variety of pastel hues. While some designs were sold simply as patterns, others came complete with the fabrics required. Some even had the required shapes already printed or stamped on the fabric, while the background contained the outline of the design elements, so the stitcher had only to cut out and position the pieces and sew them in place.

Post-war quilts

Overtly floral patterns became less widely seen in the years after World War II, when quiltmaking in general declined sharply with postwar prosperity and the unprecedented entry of women into the workplace. With much less time available for sewing and more disposable income available to many families, quiltmaking was rapidly becoming a lost art. However, throughout the 1960s a small band of dedicated quilters kept the skills of quiltmaking alive and also began to write and publish books, and to teach interested seamstresses the joys of making quilts.

By the time of the 1976 American Bicentennial, a growing number of practitioners were ready for the amazing upswing in interest in quiltmaking, and the value and historical significance of American quilts was recognized by a wider population.

BASKET OF FLOWERS

QUILT PATTERNS featuring baskets are enduringly popular. Whether they are pieced or appliquéd, they always have a reassuringly recognizable form, and they are highly versatile. Because many designs combine patchwork and appliqué, they allow the quiltmaker enormous scope for inventiveness to add flowers and other floral forms, often of her own design. They can be very simple or complex, traditional or wildly avant-garde.

Many traditional basket patterns have everyday names like Fruit Basket, Bread Basket, Tea Basket, Flowerpot, and Basket of Scraps, while others are more fanciful, such as Cakestand, Cactus Basket, and Colonial Basket. Baskets (and Houses) are among the few representational blocks used by Amish quiltmakers, and the basket pattern found most often on Amish quilts is called Amish Basket.

Baskets might be considered the quintessential folk art motif, with their simple outlines and variety of shapes. They are fun to work in appliqué as well as patchwork, and can be "filled" with all manner of creative floral designs. Most sampler quilts contain at least one basket block, and an intriguing sampler can be made entirely of a selection of basket blocks.

This Basket of Flowers quilt, a pattern sometimes known as Basket of Chips, is entirely typical of its time. Made between 1890 and 1910, it is based on a graphic two-color block turned on point and repeated in alternation with plain blue setting squares. Three rows of six basket blocks each face each other so when the quilt is placed on a bed, the baskets on the overhangs are turned the right way up.

In common with many basket patterns, this design is created almost entirely of right-angle triangles. Such patterns provide a wonderful way to use up odd scraps of fabric, because the component pieces are generally very small and using scraps provides a lively multicolored effect. However, as can be seen in this blue and white example, using just two strongly contrasting color— like navy blue and white—is highly graphic and very effective. Some examples may even look two-toned, but on close examination, the fabrics may turn out to be very slightly different versions of the same color. The blue fabric in the quilt here appears solid-colored when viewed from a distance, but in fact has a blue background with rows of quite closely spaced gray dots.

The interesting white inner border strips are 2 inches (5 cm) wide, with white corner squares. The outer borders are blue and have offset white squares adjacent to the blue corners of the inner border. The narrow binding, which is just one-quarter inch (6 mm) wide, is made from the same white muslin used on the basket blocks and for the inner border.

The quilting on basket blocks, which are frequently made from small pieces with many seams, is often quite. simple. On our example vertical and horizontal crosshatching, the lines spaced 1 inch (2.5 cm) apart, contrasts beautifully with the diamond effect creating by turning the blocks on point. The borders are quilted as one, with a 6-inch (15-cm) wide running cable that crisscrosses the seam very effectively. The batting used is cotton, as are all the other fabrics that have been utilized in this quilt.

BASKET OF FLOWERS
1890–1910

Maker unknown.
79 x 77 in.
(201 x 196 cm)

ID 1971.183.3

TREES AND FLOWERS

TREES AND FLOWERS
1910–12

Made by Christina Nicoline Nelson
Hansen, quilted by Elizabeth Moye.
97 x 92 in. (246 x 234 cm)

ID 1988.188

THE DESIGN on this intricate floral quilt is mainly appliquéd, but embroidered accents enliven the stylized motifs. The border, made of wide strips of plain cotton fabric that have been added to the top, is quilted along all four sides with simple horizontal lines.

The main applied design is of four cherry trees, with their trunks facing the edges of the quilt, their top branches almost touching along the center line. A circular motif in the exact center of the quilt perhaps represents the sun or a flower, and two birds stand guard at each tree, one on each side of the trunk. Highly stylized flowers have been placed in the four corners, as well as between each tree, and more birds fly around the flower-sun in a circle, pulling the eye around the center and out again. Flying birds also appear in the appliquéd grapevine border, replete with leaves and bunches of grapes—perhaps they are feasting on the bounty.

The quilt, which was never used, was made by Christina Nicoline Hansen between about 1910 and 1912. Her youngest son Howard Hansen, who donated the work to the Wisconsin Historical Society, remembered his mother working on this quilt, which came to him as just a top. It was quilted by Elizabeth Moye, in 1979.

Christina Hansen neé Nelson, the daughter of a Norwegian sailor and his wife, was born in 1863 in Fort Howard, Wisconsin. The quilt is finely worked, showing the obvious skill with which Mrs. Hansen, a dressmaker by profession, wielded her needle. She worked in her home state and in Oregon before marrying Hans A. Hansen, a Norwegian widower (born 1849) with three daughters. They had six children together. Mrs. Hansen died in 1947.

This floral quilt is a four-block appliqué—most of the examples of this type are floral patterns. They are generally worked on a large background square, such as the one seen here, on which each section is a 30-inch (75-cm) square of white cotton. The appliqué for the grapevine border and the central flower—or perhaps sun—and the flying birds was probably added once the four large blocks were fully completed and sewn together.

Four-block quilts are highly collectible and show great diversity in spite of being so predominantly floral. Examples of eagle motifs and Mariner's Compass designs are found, but most of the patterns on antique examples are such traditional favorites as Prince's or Princess Feather; floral wreaths; variations of myriad Rose designs from Harrison to Whig to Democratic to Mexican; and Coxcomb variations. Many are, like the example here, fairly realistic combinations of trees, flowers, birds, and other animals, and many of the designs appear to be based on motifs from chintz patterns and Tree of Life designs, both widely known at the time. The colors are very much of their time: red, green, and yellow or cheddar orange predominate, and the fabrics used are mostly solids, not prints. Elaborate borders are also seen quite often.

Other settings for large appliqué blocks are found. In some the motifs face each other, as here, while others are arranged with all the stems or trunks pointing the same way. Sometimes the blocks are turned on point, with a fifth block in the central space and triangles appliquéd with half the motif around the edges, or set with plain spacer blocks on which elaborate quilting is often worked.

NOSEGAY

PATTERNS BASED on floral bouquets abound in American folk art, not just on quilts, but on china and kitchenware, painted furniture, embroidered household linen, and all manner of decorative objects. Many nineteenth-century quilts are appliquéd with designs called Pots of Flowers, showing three or more stems of usually generic blooms growing from a vase, and most Baltimore Album quilts have at least one bouquet block, either in a holder or tied with a ribbon. A clear influence on these patterns is the printed calico, or muslin, fabric known as chintz, which often included bouquets among the designs. In the eighteenth and early nineteenth centuries, it was a common practice to cut out individual motifs from expensive chintz, both from scraps left over from a sewing project and from worn cloth, and apply them to a less costly background fabric in a technique known as broderie perse, or Persian embroidery (see page 20). Bouquets also appear on many of the lovely kit quilts that were widely made in the first half of the twentieth century (see page 20), sometimes as the central medallion that provides the focus and often as smaller motifs that appear in corners or along the sides of the quilt.

Bouquet patterns sometimes take the form of nosegays. A nosegay is a small mixture of flowers and herbs, generally sweet-smelling, that can be carried in the hand. In medieval Europe and later, nosegays called tussie-mussies were often carried by both men and women when they went outdoors, partly to distract from the pungent odors of daily life that permeated everything and partly in the belief that the sweet scents helped to ward off disease. Nosegays traditionally contain a variety of blooms, so in quiltmaking using scraps of gaily colored fabrics can make a highly effective design.

In the Nosegay quilt shown here, scraps have been used in a completely random way to create the colorful bouquets, but many of the prints used have white or pale backgrounds and the combinations of fabric are sometimes almost overpowered by the bright blue cones that contain them. This is a complex block consisting of diamond and small square scraps with a white muslin background. Two irregular triangles make up each cone. Fabrics are repeated occasionally, but the maker clearly had access to an impressive scrap basket that included checks and stripes as well as a vast assortment of brightly colored prints, some dating from much earlier than the finished quilt. Notice the bright red pieces at top left and bottom right. Were these deliberate design choices? The simple blue border, 3½ inches (9 cm) wide, matches the cones, and the piece is not quilted but simply tied with white synthetic yarn. The backing is a plain medium-blue cotton, and the edges are bound by turning the edges to the middle and then stitched by machine.

This Nosegay, also sometimes known as Bride's Bouquet, was made around 1950 by Bernice Liska Gross of Hillsboro WI and was donated to the Wisconsin Folk Museum by the maker. When that museum closed down, the collection, including the quilt, was acquired in 1966 by the State Bank of Mount Horeb, Wisconsin, and donated to the Wisconsin Historical Society.

NOSEGAY
C. 1950

Made by Bernice Liska Gross.
87 x 74 in.
(221 x 188 cm)

ID 1996.118.12

PRESIDENT'S WREATH

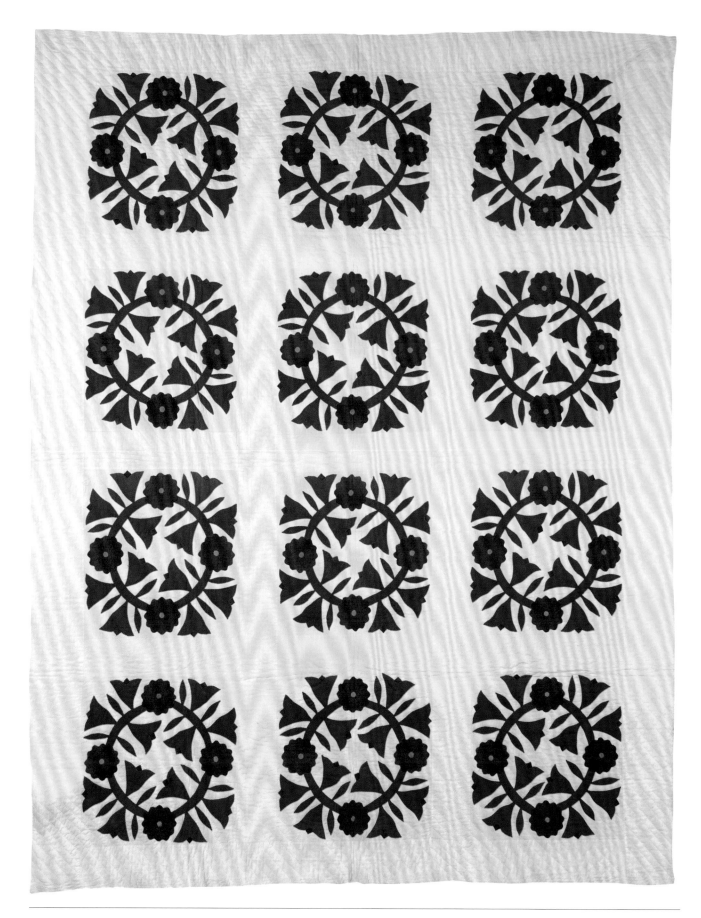

PRESIDENT'S
WREATH
1912–1914

Made by Anna Baker
Emrich (1849–1940)
for her granddaughter
Esther Emrich
Sherburne (1896–1981).
93 x 72 in.
(236 x 183 cm)

ID 2005.17.1

WREATH PATTERNS were among the most popular appliqué patterns of the nineteenth century. Many of the floral designs found on quilts of the period are arranged as a circular motif, sometimes with a central image surrounded by leaves and buds, such as the myriad Rose of Sharon designs. Wreath patterns generally have flowers, buds, and leaves in a ring with the central area left open and often quilted with a freestanding motif. In most nineteenth-century designs, the wreath's ring is closed, but a few designs have arcing sprays of flowers arranged in a circle but not touching each other.

Wreaths have long carried a religious significance, both as ritual decoration and as accessories. Brides have worn wreaths to hold their veils for centuries, and dancers celebrating the return of spring on May Day were adorned with wreaths of flowers in their hair. Wreaths appear frequently in decorative arts, from motifs painted on furniture and other household goods, to wooden carvings or plaster casts on homes and other buildings.

President's Wreath, like so many nineteenth-century block patterns, has almost as many variations as there were makers. The design was worked early in the century, but seems to have been given its name during the Civil War in tribute to President Abraham Lincoln. The red and green colors are traditional, and the pattern's popularity no doubt had much to do with the development and distribution of fabrics dyed Turkey red (see page 19), which was colorfast.

The President's Wreath shown here was made between 1912 and 1914 by Anna Baker Emrich (1849–1940) using a highly traditional version of the pattern. It was a gift for her granddaughter Esther Emrich (later Sherburne) who was attending Bushey's Appleton Business College in her hometown of Appleton, Wisconsin, from 1912 to 1914.

Mrs. Emrich was born in the town of Richfield, WI in 1849, the same year as her husband George Jacob Emrich, who was a farmer. Their son Charles Jacob (1873–1942) was the father of Esther. The quilt was donated to the Wisconsin Historical Society in 2005 by Esther's daughter Ann Sherburne Mathwig. Its pre-World War I date is quite late for such a labor-intensive quilt, and it is very lucky that Esther Sherburne and her daughter, Mrs. Mathwig, both appreciated its beauty enough to look after it well and to make sure it found its way into a public collection to be enjoyed by many people.

The flowers are red with yellow centers, while the leaves and wreath circle are green. Green flowers, perhaps lily- or bell-shaped, appear on both sides of the ring, one inside and two outside. Each has a red "stamen" that helps to create a beautiful color balance. The plain white muslin background fabric in the 17-inch (42.5-cm) blocks is also used for the wide sashing and for the borders, which are, somewhat unusually, the same width as the sashing.

The backing fabric is a blue and white polka dot that has been turned to the front to make a simple quarter-inch (6 mm) binding. Simple diagonal lines of quilting cover the entire background, running from edge to edge in only one direction.

WHOLECLOTH QUILTS

Wholecloth quilts, on which the quilting is the focus, are those made from one large piece of fabric—or so it would appear. Many wholecloth quilts are actually pieced from more than one piece of the same fabric joined in such a way as to look like a single cloth. Front and back are frequently in the same fabric, but this is not always the case. Quilting ranges from utilitarian tied yarn to highly elaborate corded and trapunto designs worked with great skill.

THE STORY OF WHOLECLOTH QUILTS

DETAIL

Pink Calamanco Wholecloth, page 38. The quilting creates a play of light across the surface of the fabric. Pieced and quilted.

ID 1963.48

DETAIL

Children's Comforter, page 40. Wholecloth quilts were often made from pieces of the same fabric joined together to look like a single piece. Pieced and tied.

ID 1990.166.3

A WHOLECLOTH quilt is not always made from a single piece of fabric. Most looms, even the very large commercial versions, did not produce a length of material that was wide enough to be used as a bedcover, so most wholecloth quilts are pieced from strips or lengths of the same fabric and then quilted in an overall design that makes the seams virtually disappear.

The first quilts used as bedcovers were probably lengths of plain fabric joined to make a piece that could extend across the bed with adequate overhang. Most examples avoid a distracting seam down the center, so strips are sewn along each side of a central full-width piece. These tops were batted and backed and held together with some form of stitching or tying. The quilting provides texture in the quilt and allows a play of light across the surface that gives these quilts their beauty.

British wholecloths

Early examples are not always finely worked, but by the nineteenth century, wholecloth quilts were among the most highly prized of many a household's possessions. Wholecloth quilting was widely practiced in Great Britain, especially in Ireland and Wales, where antique wholecloth quilts predominate. These quilts were generally made from wool cloth, and the batting is also wool of a fine, well-combed grade. The batting made the closely worked quilting a necessity, since the padding shifted very easily as the quilt was used and cleaned, and if tiny quilting stitches were worked across it in narrowly spaced patterns, the batting had less chance of moving around inside the quilt.

The northeastern border counties of Durham and Northumberland in England were also famous for their wholecloth quilts. As wool was

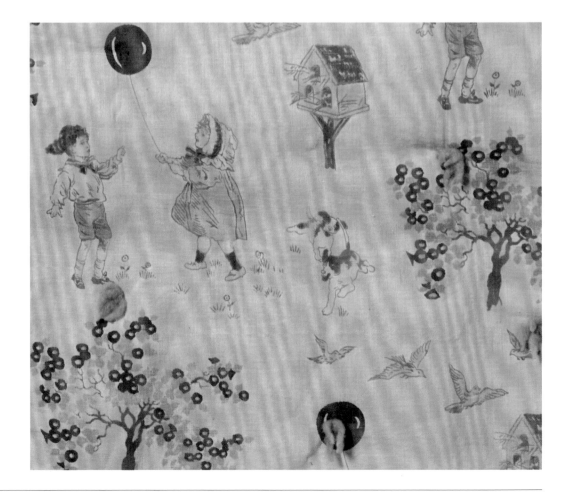

overtaken by finer, more closely woven cottons like poplin and sateen, Durham quilting, as it became known, became famous, and many of the most beautiful of nineteenth-century wholecloth quilts were made in this area. The economy of the area where these quilts were made depended heavily on coal mining, a precarious and often dangerous way to make a living. The area is remote and isolated, a far cry from the bustling commercial centers and industrial areas of the country like London, Liverpool, and Manchester. In the urban centers there was a growing and affluent middle class willing to purchase goods that had previously been made at home—bedcovers among them—while in the Northeast there were plenty of talented quiltmakers, both men and women, who could earn extra income by making quilts for city folk.

By the early 1800s, quiltmaking in Northeast England had developed into a cottage industry that lasted into the twentieth century. Miner's wives and widows were the main practitioners of the craft, and quilt clubs formed, with weekly subscriptions—similar to today's layaway plans—paid by prospective customers, who then received their quilt when the price was paid in full. A substantial number of so-called Durham quilts can be found today in museums and private collections, a testament to both their artistic and historical value.

Among the Durham quilters were a group of itinerants, mainly men, who traveled the countryside exchanging bed and board for quiltmaking in households affluent enough to be able to pay for the warm bedcovers they needed. The most famous traveling quilter was Joseph Hedley, known as Joe the Quilter. He was renowned in his lifetime as a quiltmaker of extraordinary skill, and it is assumed that many people in the area thought he had made a relative fortune for his work. He retired to a small thatched cottage near the village of Warden in Northumberland, where he was brutally

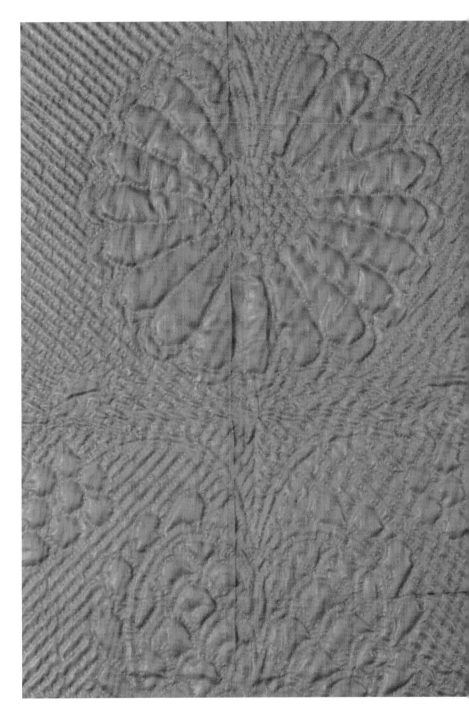

DETAIL

Pink Calamanco Wholecloth, page 38. Calamanco is a worsted wool fabric that has been glazed, and it was considered highly desirable for quiltmaking.
Pieced and quilted.

ID 1963.48

DETAIL

Trapunto Wholecloth Quilt, page 36. Most wholecloth quilts have a central motif that is echoed in the corners or borders.
Quilted and stuffed.

ID 1949.162

murdered sometime between January 3 and 7 of 1826. The crime was thought to be the work of robbers, but no one was ever arrested or charged. The shocking circumstances served to increase his celebrity, and his fame lives on, in spite of the fact that only a handful of quilts that can be verified as his work survive.

In addition to the "club quilters" and the itinerants, there was another group of professional quiltmakers, known as stampers, who drew an appropriate design on a quilt top in blue pencil for a customer to quilt herself. Marked tops could be purchased or special-ordered from the company, and peddlers who traveled in the rural areas sometimes carried marked tops in their packs to sell. The most famous stampers were George Gardiner and one of his apprentices, Elizabeth Sanderson. Both taught their skills to numerous apprentices, and many of the traditional patterns they devised and passed on in their work survive to this day.

American wholecloths

As the United States grew from its original thirteen states throughout the 1800s, quiltmaking traditions traveled with its people, and the wholecloth quilting ideas and designs that had been brought by the early settlers were adapted and refined. In colonial North America, weaving and clothmaking were discouraged, lest a homegrown product interfere with the lucrative British weaving trade that was centered around the cities of Manchester and Liverpool. After independence, and with the decline of the industry in England, cloth merchants immigrated to the United States and began to create versions of chintz patterns that became very popular in quiltmaking. Chintz is a type of cotton cloth, originally woven and printed in India, that became wildly popular in Europe and then in North America, and a number of colonial and Early American examples of wholecloth chintz quilts survive, including some with motifs celebrating, in 1876, the centenary of the birth of the country.

Quilting designs

The most desirable wholecloth quilts are hand quilted and the variety of patterns is limitless. Many of the most popular designs appear to originate with the Durham quilters and have been adapted and elaborated upon by quiltmakers everywhere. Designs were exchanged among friends and relations, and also copied from old quilts. Most wholecloth quilts have a central motif that is then echoed in the corners. Simple geometric quilting, such as crosshatching or fans, enhances the more elaborate center, and wide border patterns often appear on the edges. Many of the border designs are worked on three sides, giving the quilt a simpler area to go at the head of the bed.

Tied quilts are more utilitarian and were almost invariably for everyday (or every night) use. They are often thickly batted, making quilting by hand somewhat challenging. Tying a quilt with yarn, thread, ribbon, or string at intervals can be accomplished much more quickly than a design that had to be quilted with tiny stitches and close-set rows.

TRAPUNTO WHOLECLOTH QUILT

ONE OF THE oldest European quilts still in existence is known as the Tristan quilt. Housed in London's Victoria & Albert Museum, it is thought to have been made in Italy in the sixteenth century using a technique known as Italian quilting, or trapunto. Its mate, an Isolde quilt, which may have been half of the original, has not been found.

The quilt may have been lost, but the technique has not. It involves sewing two layers together by outlining design areas and inserting lengths of cord or small amounts of padding to enhance the design and give a three-dimensional effect to the surface of the quilt. The method has grown in popularity recently as new techniques, including machine trapunto, have been developed, and this three-dimensional work is known by several different names depending on how the effect is created. Cording, or Italian cording, is accomplished by stitching a narrow channel and then threading cord or yarn through it. This method works beautifully for stems, vines, and garlands, and is sometimes worked as side-by-side channels to create a densely padded background of furrows.

Larger shapes can be stuffed through openings in the back of the work, which are slipstitched closed and covered with the quilt's batting and backing. These openings can be cut if the backing fabric is tightly woven, while if a loosely woven cloth such as a quality cheesecloth is used, the threads can be teased apart and then realigned after the padding is in place. Areas of appliqué are sometimes filled with stuffing, either by inserting the padding through a small slit cut in the background fabric, which is then whipstitched to close it, or just before the final stitches that attach the applied piece to the background fabric are made.

The fringed whitework quilt shown here was made in the traditional way, by hand, in the 1840s, at a time when such quilts were referred to as "stuffed work." In spite of some staining the execution and condition of its quilting are very fine examples of its type. The central area of the quilt is a basket of flowers. It has no handle, and the basket itself is created with cording to make the base, the scalloped rim, and the basketweave sides. Flowers, especially tulips, and leaves, corded and stuffed, spill from the basket, which is surrounded by a ring of beautifully executed stuffed feathers. A rectangular medallion panel, its corners filled with stuffed flowers, leaves, and bunches of grapes, is delineated by a double running feather, also stuffed. The area between the panel and the outside edges is decorated with a looping curvaceous garland of flowers and leaves, which are like the rest of the piece, worked in cording and stuffing. One half of the feather motif that is used on the ring around the central basket has been repeated side by side along the outside edges, making a splendid stitched "border" around the quilt.

The handmade white cotton fringe appears on all four sides. Each set of threads crosses its neighbors twice before being tied and teased out along the edge, and it is caught in between the top and the back, in the edges-to-middle binding.

TRAPUNTO WHOLECLOTH QUILT 1840–1845

Maker unknown.
104 x 96 in.
(264 x 244 cm)

ID 1949.162

Pink Calamanco Wholecloth

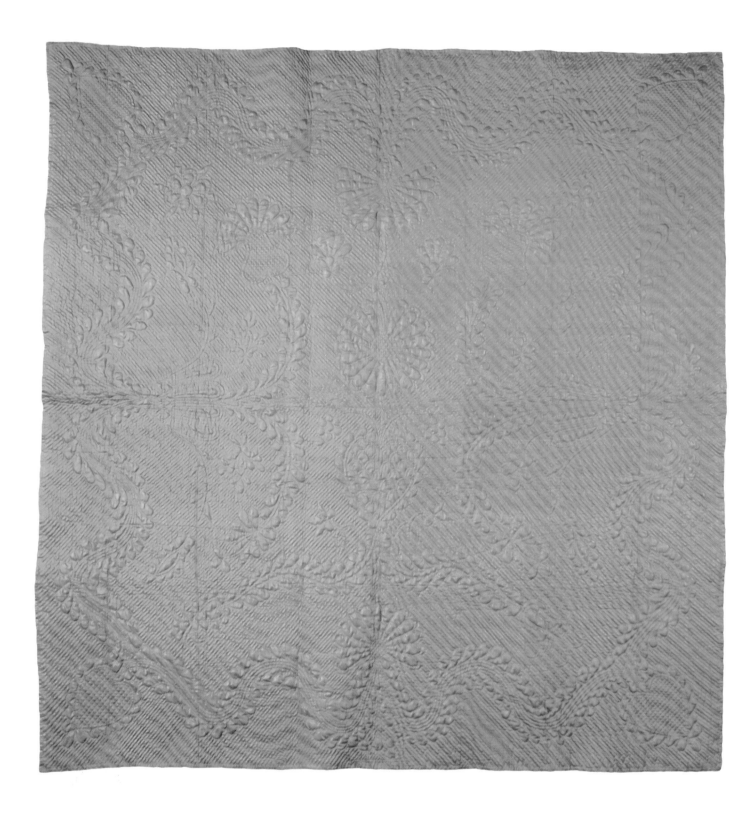

PINK CALAMANCO
WHOLECLOTH
C. 1800

Maker unknown.
90 x 88 in.
(230 x 225 cm)

ID 1963.48

CALAMANCO, or calimanco, is a quality worsted wool fabric woven in a plain (satin) or twill weave. Made in the eighteenth and nineteenth centuries, it differs from other woolens in that it was glazed, or polished, under pressure and heat, a method known as calendering. It was generally woven in a medium weight, and was considered highly desirable for making quilted bedcovers. Colors were deep, rich solids, as well as checks and stripes, and a definition from Webster's 1828 dictionary calls it simply "a woolen stuff, of a fine gloss, and checkered in the warp."

It was often used to make the tops of wholecloth quilts in colonial North America and in the years following the American Revolution. Existing examples are usually solid colored, and most display skillfully worked and elaborate quilting patterns. The batting is almost invariably wool as well, while the backs are made from rougher stuff, sometimes a lower-quality wool, homespun, or a fabric known as linsey-woolsey. The latter term covers a number of wool fabrics, many of which had a linen, and later cotton, warp thread. The name was eventually applied to encompass almost all of the wool fabrics used in many wholecloth quilts made during the era, but a goodly number of these should more accurately be called calamanco.

The top of this calamanco "wholecloth" is actually pieced from strips approximately 24 inches (60 cm) wide, and has a beautifully worked large-scale floral and feather design. The batting and backing are both wool as well, with the backing pieced from a green and white homespun check about 10 inches (25 cm) wide along the sides and a central panel of brown linsey-woolsey. The quilting patterns are traditional, with a typical central area that includes a floral design and a heart-shaped motif surrounded by an elaborate running feather pattern that dips in and out in a roughly rectangular shape.

Each of the four corners of the quilt has a pointed oval motif, and all are joined by a running feather border that echoes but does not copy the center one. Floral designs appear at intervals around the border, some part of the border feather pattern, others freestanding. Fine diagonal lines approximately a quarter of an inch (6 mm) apart fill every area of the background outside the motifs, giving the quilt dramatic textural effects that are highlighted by the sheen provided by the glazed fabric. Another typical aspect is the binding, in which the front and back edges of the quilt are turned to the middle and stitched in place.

Most calamancos were made in New England, which was the most settled area of the continent, and finding an example as fine as this magnificent bright pink wholecloth in the Midwest means that it almost certainly came west as part of a pioneer household. Hearts were generally incorporated into the designs on bridal quilts, so the inclusion of the single heart in the center motif may indicate that this quilt came to the Midwest along with a newlywed couple who were starting life away from their original homes.

Children's Comforter

CHILDREN'S
COMFORTER
1920–1929

Maker unknown.
59 x 50¼ in.
(150 x 128 cm)

ID 1990.166.3

MANY WHOLECLOTH quilts are simple comforters, made quickly for everyday use. Some are stitched, while others, like this charming utilitarian example, are batted thickly for warmth and tied. Both the size and the pattern of the print make it likely that this was a quilt made for a child's bed.

The top and backing are in the same cotton fabric and are joined from large pieces that are likely to have originated as feedsacks. No attempt has been made to match the pattern repeats, but the overall impact is still consistent. The colors have probably faded over time, but the boy in his shorts, sailor shirt, and coonskin cap and the girl in her simple dress and elaborate bonnet tied under the chin are still very eye-catching and appealing. Two brown and white puppies run around in the grass nearby, and a flock of birds of indeterminate color fly away from the dogs and toward the birdhouse. Trees full of red fruit—or perhaps they are flowers—complete the delightful scene.

The tying that holds the quilt together has been worked in turquoise cotton thread and is randomly spaced, but a number of the ties have been placed in the center of some of the red balloons that the girl is holding, emphasizing the shapes. The edge-to-middle binding is stitched by machine. The entire effect is of a happy, cuddly way to keep warm and snuggled up in bed.

Feedsacks were widely used from the 1920s through the '40s for making items of clothing, household linen, and especially quilts. Many dry food items, both for animals, especially chickens, and humans—such staples as flour, sugar, cornmeal, and other grains, as well as seeds—had for many years been packed in cloth bags for distribution. The larger bags that carried feed and seed were to be found on every farm in the United States, and smaller bags of foodstuffs were standard in every kitchen. Originally they were made of plain cotton, sometimes printed with the name of the company that processed or packaged the product. Quilts are found that have backing made from whole sacks pieced together, and feedsacks frequently were used in patchwork tops, but generally the printed logos and information were removed when the patches were cut. In order to entice customers to buy substantial amounts of a particular product, bags began to be printed with patterns similar to the bright, cheerful ones on the fabrics found in stores. A quilter could choose bags in desirable prints and when the sack was empty, she could combine them to make her quilt. Anna Eelman, in an article for *The Quilters' Ultimate Visual Guide*, credits Richard Peck of the Percy Kent Bag Company with being the first to see the potential, and he signed up well-known designers for his company's bags. Other companies saw the point, and soon the printed cloth bags were ubiquitous.

Millions of yards of printed cotton fabric were used to make feedsacks, and many of those lengths and pieces of cloth ended up in quilts. Most American children who were born during the Great Depression through to the end of World War II wore something—from underwear to shirts, shorts, and skirts to Sunday dresses—made from feedsacks, as well as sleeping under quilts made from them.

EMBELLISHED QUILTS

Art quilts today are essentially an extension of the embellished quilts of yesteryear. The most popular form of embellishment is, of course, embroidery, which is found particularly on Victorian crazy quilts. Embroidery has also been used on many other types of quilts to adorn appliqué motifs, add a touch of brightness to somber fabrics, and even as the motif itself on cross-stitched and redwork quilts. Many folk art quilts are decorated with embellishments that add greatly to their charm and liveliness.

THE STORY OF EMBELLISHED QUILTS

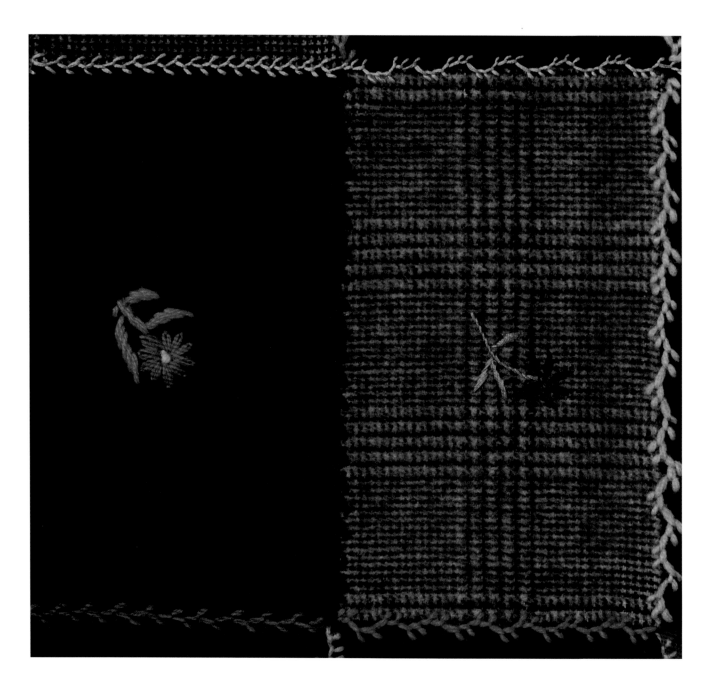

DETAIL

Embroidered Wool Lap
Quilt, page 54.
Unwanted sample
books were often a
good source of fabric
for quilts.
Embroidered: multi-
color on black, gray,
and brown.

ID 1996.118.6

THE EMBELLISHMENT of textiles is an ancient art, practiced by many civilizations. Chinese embroidery dates back thousands of years, and in the Middle East craftsmen from Egypt and Assyria to Babylonia and Persia lavished embellishments on their textiles, both garments and household goods, ceremonial and utilitarian. Many of the techniques traveled along the Silk Road, or from the Indus valley, to reach Europe and become an influence there on medieval and renaissance textiles, particularly clothing and church vestments and decorations. African tribes decorated garments and ceremonial robes with stitchery, beads, and feathers, as did civilizations like the Incas, the Aztecs, and the Mayas in the western hemisphere.

By the seventeenth century in Europe, embellishment could be found not just on clothing but on all manner of household textiles, including hangings and curtains for beds, windows, and doors. Appliqué and quilting, together with patchwork, are considered to be embroidery techniques, and their appearance on garments—often combined with surface embroidery—became widespread. The techniques were carried to the American colonies, where they were used to make quilts and bed covers that became in their turn subjects for embellishment. By the middle of the nineteenth century, elaborate embellishment appeared on many quilts both in the United States and Europe, particularly in Great Britain during the long reign of Queen Victoria.

Crazy Quilts

The best-known group of embellished quilts is without a doubt the Crazy Quilts so beloved of genteel Victorian quiltmakers on both sides of the Atlantic, often made from scraps of fine fabric.

The silks, brocades, taffetas, and velvets found in examples of crazy quilts from the era were probably left over from dressmaking, and many of the quiltmakers who can be identified were indeed dressmakers. Crazy quilts are also found made from and decorated with wool, and from cotton, but these, while charming, lack the elegance and intensity of their more sophisticated sisters. They are also more likely to be of a later date, and made in rural areas. The elaborate quilts of Victoriana were designed mainly to show off the maker's skills with a needle, and were more likely to be intended as throws or lap quilts in the parlor than being used as bedcovers.

Crazy quilts were sewn together in odd-shaped pieces to give a higgledy-piggledy effect. Almost all Victorian crazy quilts were pieced by mounting the fabric scraps on a foundation backing, and—particularly in American quilts—

DETAIL

Redwork Quilt, page 50. Surface embroidery has long been a popular way to embellish quilts. Embroidered: red on white.

ID 1968.563.2

DETAIL

Crazy Quilt With Fans,
page 52. Crazy quilts
were usually made in
luxurious fabrics to
demonstrate the
maker's skill, so many
good examples have
survived.
Pieced and
embroidered.

ID 2004.134.2

these backings are often cut into good-sized squares. Once the foundation is covered with scraps, it can be trimmed and joined to other similar squares until a quilt of the desired size has been put together. Called "contained crazy" construction, the method differs from the mainly British technique, in which the scraps are applied to a large backing to make one large piece.

In both methods the embellishment comes after the top is full size. A variety of decorative embroidery stitches can be found on most crazy quilts, from the most popular—feather stitch—to cross-stitch, chain stitch, and herringbone stitch, to name but a few. These border stitches are used to outline each individual piece of fabric in the quilt. Many of the larger scraps of fabric

are decorated further, with motifs, usually pictorial, embroidered, or in some cases drawn or painted, on them. Other examples have delightful appliqué work, which is itself often further embellished with embroidery or beadwork. Among the most popular designs were owls (a symbol of wisdom), butterflies and other insects, birds and other animals, plants and flowers of all kinds, fans, and horseshoes for luck. The designs often were commercial patterns, either iron-on transfers or stitched patches, but many were designed and drafted by the quiltmaker or a friend. The embroidered decoration served to ornament the quilt, but also to stabilize the pieces and to hide the seams or the raw edges between each piece. Most crazy quilts were not quilted, but relied on the density of the decorative stitching to hold the piece together, though quilted examples are found, usually with tied quilting. Many crazy quilts were signed and/or dated by their makers, which has been a boon to quilt historians.

Redwork and Cross-stitch Quilts

Toward the end of the nineteenth century and into the twentieth, a fashion for embroidered quilts developed. Though embroidery appears on quilts to some extent throughout their history, both on crazy quilts and signature quilts (see pages 56–68), the use of an embroidered motif as the only design element first became popular in the 1880s. By the turn of the century, patterns could be readily purchased as squares of plain cotton fabric, known as "penny squares," printed or stamped with an outline design. Many quiltmakers used simple line drawings of the type found in children's books, or published in magazines for the purpose, to draft their own squares. Most of these blocks were worked as Redwork, in which simple straight-line embroidery like stem stitch was used to outline the motif. The term redwork comes from the fact that most of these quilts were stitched in red thread, though other colors, mainly blue, but occasionally green or brown and even black, are sometimes found. Some examples are worked in multicolors, especially those made for children. Perhaps because the work itself is delicate, embroidered quilts are seldom heavy in weight, and they generally display unambitious quilting patterns, usually simple crosshatching. In fact, many of them are not quilted at all, but simply backed for use as summer coverlets.

The motifs on redwork and other embroidered quilts provide clues to their dates. Designs found on the early examples are similar to the popular motifs used on the crazy quilts of the period, while themed blocks—alphabets, nursery rhymes, state birds or flowers, for example—appeared several decades later. Historical events are often depicted, and provide a fairly accurate way of dating a quilt. Many of these blocks were produced commercially to commemorate particular occasions, such as a territory being granted statehood, or to depict famous people from history. A later craze for cross-stitch quilts hit the country in the 1920s. Most of the examples were available as kits that included the quilt fabric stamped with the design and also the thread needed to complete all the embroidery. Redwork was less popular in Britain than in the US, despite the fact that it was an English firm, William Briggs Company, which developed an iron-on transfer that was used to place a design on fabric.

Today's quiltmakers, especially art quilters, use embellishment to enhance their work. Beads, feathers, buttons, and other traditional objects often appear, together with ribbons, cords, and lace and all manner of decorative threads. Items such as pieces of jewelry or charms that have a personal meaning are used to create texture or provide a symbolic message.

DETAIL

Embroidered Silk Fair Ribbons, page 48. Silk ribbons were often printed with motifs or slogans and could be further embellished with embroidery. Pieced and embroidered: gold on red and blue.

ID 1996.118.1

EMBROIDERED SILK FAIR RIBBONS

EMBROIDERED SILK
FAIR RIBBONS
C. 1915

Maker unknown;
Wisconsin-Illinois
border.
76½ x 63 in.
(194 x 160 cm)

ID 1996.118.14

A GOOD NUMBER of known quilts that are embellished with embroidery are made from silk. Not only would silk have been easy to stitch, it would also have been a pleasure to hold while working. Silk ribbons have been used in quilts since the Victorian fashion for making quilts from fancy fabrics began. There are Log Cabin quilts made entirely from ribbons—think how easy the task would be if the strips were already cut. Silk and velvet ribbons appear in crazy quilts galore, especially to carry a signature or a date. Ribbons were employed to make fan blades and appliquéd as decoration for many folk art quilts, and cotton and flannel ribbons were also used.

Tobacco smoking, a widespread male pastime by the late nineteenth century, provided a source of free fabric for quiltmakers in cigar flannels and ribbons, and cigarette silks, called silkies, that were printed with themed designs. The silk ribbons carried series such as birds and animals, flowers, and famous historical figures. Flags of nations were also widely found, especially on cigar flannels. These printed ribbons are found incorporated into quilts of the late nineteenth century, while ribbons commemorating political or historical events were also popular with quiltmakers.

Another type of ribbon that turns up in quilts are the colored ribbons, usually made of silk, that were presented to prize winners of all types from county and state fairs, where judges evaluated everything from pies and preserves to cattle, sheep, and poultry. And of course quilts. Ribbons were awarded to children who won spelling bees and yodeling contests. First prize was blue, second was red, and third white, with honorable mentions generally yellow, though sometimes the honorables were white and third was yellow.

Because they were bright and colorful, as well as very important mementoes of a person's accomplishments, these ribbons often found their way into quilts.

The ribbons used to make this quilt top are silk satin ribbons, presented as prizes at county agricultural fairs in Illinois and Wisconsin in 1913 and 1914. Each one is printed in gold with the appropriate official state seal and bears an inscription saying either "McHENRY COUNTY FAIR/WOODSTOCK, ILL.–1913" or "–1914" or "BIG ROCK COUNTY FAIR/EVANSVILLE, WIS.–1913" or "–1914." The ribbons were perhaps left unused and acquired by an unknown quiltmaker, who put them together around 1915 into eighty square blocks. Each block is made from four ribbons, two each of blue—first place, or "FIRST PREMIUM"—and two of red for "SECOND PREMIUM" alternating side by side. They are mounted on black foundation backing squares and secured with decorative stitching done in yellow-gold embroidery thread. The blocks are then combined in such a way that the ribbons run alternately vertically and horizontally to create a basic rail fence pattern.

A number of outline and border stitches have been used for the embellishment. Herringbone and feather stitch, both single and double feather, appear most often, and occasionally there is a row of triple feather stitch. A delightful chicken foot stitch alternates direction on some rows. The edges of the blocks are embellished with embroidery in the same way that the rows are stitched, creating an overall effect of vitality and a certain opulence that can be found only with silk as it changes color when it catches the light. The top was never finished.

Redwork Quilt

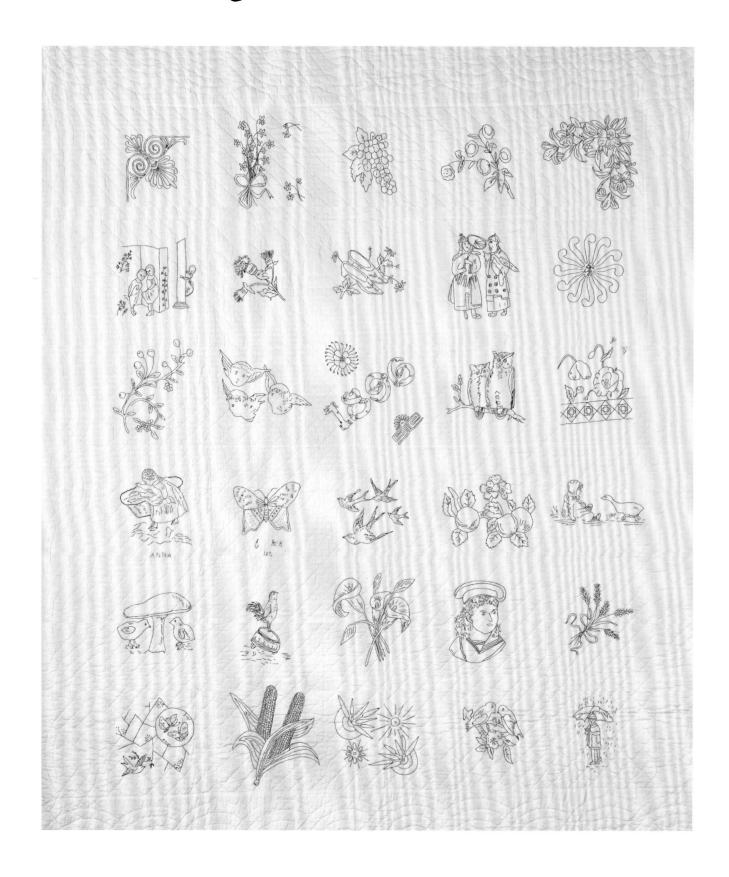

REDWORK QUILT
1896

Made by Anna M. Hoyt
Wells (b. 1838?, death
date unknown);
Fond du Lac,
Wisconsin.
80 x 67 in.
(203 x 170 cm)

ID 1968.563.2

REDWORK IS an embroidery technique that has been used on quilts since the last quarter of the nineteenth century. Embroidery has been used to decorate American quilts since as early as the eighteenth century, but until the popularity of redwork took hold it was used mainly for embellishing designs, often appliqué but pieced work as well. The use of embroidery alone as the main design element on a quilt was a new idea, and it became fashionable—especially for quilts made for babies and children, but also for signature and friendship quilts (see pages 56–69).

Most redwork is worked as stem stitch, or backstitch, to outline the motif with no in-filling. Red stranded floss is far and away the most popular thread used, although there are quilts stitched with blue, or even green, yellow, and black. The popularity of the red thread is tied to the widespread availability of floss dyed with a colorfast dye known as Turkey red (see page 19) by the late 1800s. The other important technological advance that influenced the interest in redwork was the development of a transfer that could easily be ironed on the background fabric. Previous methods for transferring pattern to cloth, such as stencils, were laborious, and some, like pouncing chalk through a series of holes in a perforated pattern, were messy as well. In 1874, William Briggs Company in Britain developed a process in which a reversed design motif could be transferred to fabric by ironing it with a hot iron, and within a short time both transfer patterns and individual preprinted squares were available commercially.

Most redwork quilts are made from individual blocks that are joined either edge to edge or with sashing, which is almost invariably red or red and white. Many of these blocks were preprinted "penny squares," first introduced at the Pan-American Exposition held in Buffalo, New York, in 1901, which could be purchased either singly or in sets. On early redwork quilts the motifs tended to be similar to the designs used to embellish the crazy quilts (see pages 45–47) that were all the rage at the time. Fans, horseshoes, and owls were particularly favored, as well as flowers, butterflies and other insects, and also birds and animals. Themed quilts soon became very popular, featuring everything from the elaborate designs of British artist Kate Greenaway, whose charming drawings of children were instantly recognizable, to state flowers, or farm animals, or the days of the week.

The quilt featured here was made by Anna M. Hoyt Wells, who was born around 1838 in Massachusetts. Her family moved to Wisconsin around 1855, and in 1892 she married a farmer-turned-banker John C. Wells (1821–1899). Her redwork quilt is dated 1896 (in the middle of the third row). The piece features a variety of delightful motifs, from ears of corn and a sheaf of wheat to various flowers, an owl and other birds, shoes, and even a man standing under an umbrella in the rain. The Japanese couple seen in the second row is a typically popular motif of the time, when all things oriental became the rage, following their introduction through the Great Exposition at the Crystal Palace in London in 1851 and the American Centennial Exposition in Philadelphia in 1876. The blocks are joined edge to edge and quilted with a simple crosshatch grid, with a triple cable pattern in the plain wide outside border.

CRAZY QUILT WITH FANS

WHILE THERE were undoubtedly many early quilts and garments made by sewing small scraps together in a random fashion, the resulting pattern—the crazy quilt—as we know it is a High Victorian invention. Thousands of crazy quilts have survived since the fad's heyday in the last quarter of the nineteenth century, in part because they were not utilitarian but created to show the maker's needlework skills. The majority of known examples are made from silk, velvet, satin, and other fine fabrics, which means that they were looked after more carefully than workaday cotton and wool quilts designed to be used as bedcovers, which would have been laundered at least occasionally.

Many Victorian-era crazy quilts were made as memorials to departed loved ones and might have included pieces of clothing or other textiles that belonged to them. Others were made as gifts to mark significant occasions such as a marriage or christening. Scraps of fabric were laid on foundation blocks, usually squares, and basted in place. Raw edges were turned under and seamed with decorative embroidery stitches that were worked through the backing, though in some cases pieces were sewn to the foundation in a stitch-and-flip method and the resulting seams embellished with fancy stitches. The beautiful embroidery found on many pieces in crazy quilts could be done either before the pieces were joined or alternatively when the decorative seaming was being worked.

Crazy quilts were made in all regions of the United States, where the citizens followed trends from abroad, particularly Britain. British crazy quilts are usually arranged around a decorated center square, which often has the name of the maker and the date embroidered or inscribed on it. The center is then surrounded by areas of crazy patchwork in a form similar to the older medallion, or frame, quilts that were popular in the eighteenth and early nineteenth century. A number of American quilts were arranged this way, but more often quiltmakers in the United States worked on foundation squares which were then combined to make an entire quilt. This method, known as contained crazy or crazy block pattern, has been used for the quilt here, although the squares are somewhat smaller than usually found.

Minnie Levene Spencer Germond (1862–1936) made this fascinating example of a crazy quilt, probably between 1882 and 1886. Her maiden-name initials "M.L.S." appear on the band of brown silk just below the bottom of the fan, and "1884" in a black triangle under the monogram. There are fifty square crazy blocks, and they are unusual in being set on point. Smaller square blocks, sometimes made from only two fabrics, have been used to fill in the edges, creating a chevron design that is bound in beige silk. Most of the larger squares contain at least one embroidered scrap, and some fabrics have a date written on them. These appear to be scraps from wedding dresses inscribed with the date of the marriage, including Minnie's mother's 1856 gown. Minnie married Harry Johnson Germond (1859–1936) in 1886, after the quilt was finished, and no one knows if scraps from her own dress were included.

CRAZY QUILT WITH FANS
1882–1886

Made by Minnie Levene Spencer Germond (1862–1936); Fond du Lac, Wisconsin.
60 1/2 x 58 3/4 in. (154 x 149 cm)

ID 2004.134.2

Embroidered Wool Lap Quilt

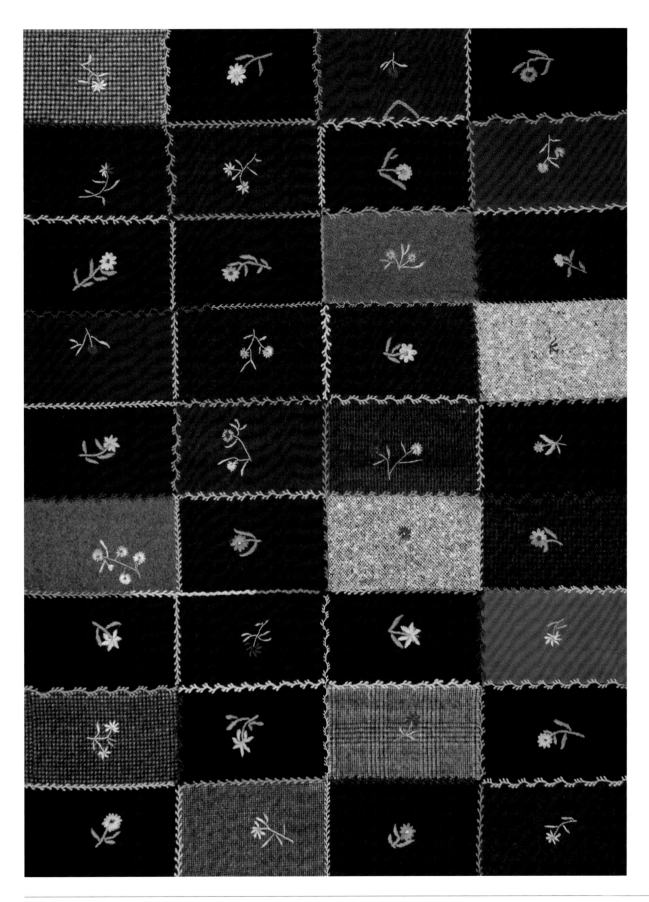

EMBROIDERED
WOOL LAP QUILT
1900–1940

Made by Dina, Emma,
and/or Clara Olson;
Seneca Township,
Wisconsin.
43½ x 32¼ in.
(110 x 82 cm)

ID 1996.118.6

Plaid wool twill has
been used for the
backing of the quilt.

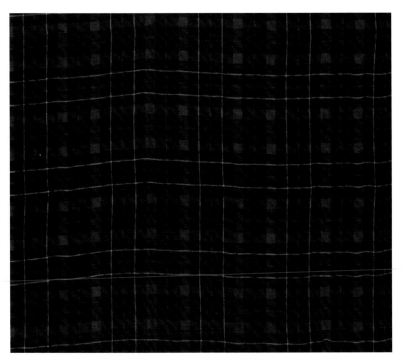

QUILTERS GENERALLY prefer to work with natural fibers. On the whole, they are easier to work with than synthetics, and almost always are nicer to handle. Wool and cotton have been quilters' favorites for hundreds of years, for their ease of sewing and their ability to hold dye, as well as their variety in weight and weave.

Wool cloth comes in two forms. Ordinary wool is spun from short-staple fleece that has been carded. Worsted comes from fleece with a long staple and has been combed. Both are warm, strong, and elastic, but have a tendency to shrink. All wool holds dye well, giving rich, dark colors to the fabric. Wool is, however, thick and rough, while worsted is smooth, firm, and much finer. It also has a sheen and is widely used in men's suits.

Many early quilts in Great Britain and North American were made of wool, and in many cases were batted with wool as well. Beautiful wholecloth and medallion quilts made in Wales and Scotland in the early nineteenth century are fashioned from wool or from calamanco, a glazed wool that was also popular in the American colonies (see page 38), and wool quilts were widely made throughout the nineteenth century and into the early 1900s.

Military quilts, also known as soldier quilts, are almost always made of wool. This group of quilts, made by mainly British military personnel in the mid-nineteenth century, were often sewn by the tailors who accompanied the British army wherever it went. Using scraps and remnants of the wool melton that was used to make uniforms, these quiltmakers created highly geometric patterns, often containing hundreds of carefully crafted and stitched patches. Some of the resulting quilts were used as blankets and ground covers by personnel in the field, while others were worked as memorials to the fallen or for ceremonial use, and a surprising number of them have survived.

By the late nineteenth century some lucky quiltmakers were taking advantage of sample books of fabric that were carried by sales representatives for cloth manufacturers, who traveled from place to place to sell their wares. When a new line, or range, of fabric was introduced, the old sample books might not be needed, and their contents, already cut into small pieces that were often all the same size, sometimes found their way into quilts. Books of wool suiting samples were among these treasures, and it is possible that the thirty-six rectangular patches in this lap quilt began life in such a fashion. Each 5- by 8-inch (12.5- by 20-cm) patch has been embellished with an embroidered flower. The delicate and colorful flowers and multicolored decorative feather stitching on the seams contrast wonderfully with the somber colors of the cloth.

This quilt was made by women of the Olson family—Dina and/or a daughter, either Clara or Emma—sometime between 1900 and 1940. The plaid backing is also wool: a teal, navy, black, red, and yellow twill. The embroidery has been worked in wool yarn and pearl cotton, and the quilt is tied with navy blue thread, with the ties on the back. The binding is edges to middle.

SIGNATURE QUILTS

Adding a signature to a card or a letter is a way of giving a personal greeting to the recipient. Signature quilts have been used for nearly two centuries to send warm wishes and comforting thoughts to those who use the quilt. Some were made for a person or family and signed by their friends and relatives, to commemorate a special occasion or to wish them "godspeed" in a new phase of their lives. Others were signed by members of a community to raise money for a worthy cause.

AMONG THE most charming American quilts are those bearing signatures. These enigmatic documents are found across the country, most signed by anonymous citizens, long deceased, and in far too many cases the history behind the quilts is lost forever. Signature quilts are not the same as signed quilts, when the maker signs—and hopefully dates—a quilt on the back, much like any artist signs a painting.

Signature quilts are known by several names. They are often called album quilts, and sometimes referred to as friendship quilts or autograph quilts. Album quilts fall into a larger category, exemplified by an extraordinary group of quilts made between about 1840 and 1860 in and around Baltimore, Maryland (see page 20). These beautifully executed bedcovers comprised a set of appliqué blocks that were generally pictorial and often floral. Many of them were signed and dated on the front by the maker of the quilt, or by individual block makers, a practice that has been extraordinarily helpful to historians, both generalists and those particularly interested in the history of quilts, and which allows us to be uncharacteristically precise about the dates and places relating to these quilts. Many crazy quilts, most made later in the nineteenth century, were also signed and dated, but they were seldom made by a group of people working together, while a number of the Baltimore quilts were executed by several makers, who usually worked to a planned design.

Friendship quilts

Some signature quilts are perhaps more accurately called friendship quilts. The quilts in this group were usually given as presents to friends or relatives to commemorate an auspicious event, or more likely as a parting gift to a pastor or school master transferring to another location or a family moving west. A significant number of the signature quilts that are known today were made early in the nineteenth century, a time when large-scale migration was taking place as the lands west of the Appalachian Mountains and then beyond the Mississippi River were being explored and opened up to new settlement. Newlywed couples and families, as well as intrepid individual pioneers looking for a better or more exciting life, joined in the westward movement, which didn't stop until it reached the Pacific Ocean. Travel could only be accomplished on horseback, in covered wagons, or on river boats, and the amount of goods that could be transported was limited, so any gift that was useful as well as beautiful, and which allowed the pioneers to take with them a little piece of the home they were leaving and something of the people who were staying behind, was treasured. As a result, a significant number of these heirlooms have survived. Certainly the warmth provided by quilts would have been welcomed in many of the places settled by the pioneers, with frigid winter temperatures and deep, long-lasting snow cover a fact of life on the vast plains that make up the landscape from the Mississippi River to the Rocky Mountains.

Fundraiser Quilts

Many of the quilts that bear signatures have a large number of names. Quite a few of the examples that have a known history, especially among those dating from the last quarter of the 1800s, were made as fund raisers, often for a local church or other community institution. Blocks were sometimes made by one quilter and made available to members of the community to sign, which they usually did in ink. These inked autographs were sometimes then embroidered, usually by one or two stitchers who could execute the work skillfully. This meant that people who couldn't sew could take part in the effort.

Some of the examples were clearly made by a number of people, and often each block was signed by its own maker. In some cases, each signer paid to have his or her name included.

Many of these quilts were presented to a local
dignitary—the minister at the church, the mayor
upon his retirement—and the funds that had been
raised went to repair the sanctuary roof or to build
an addition to the town hall, perhaps. Others were
made to promote a cause, and members of the
Woman's Christian Temperance Union, founded
in 1874 to fight the evils of alcohol and its
detrimental effect on society, were among the
most prolific quiltmakers of the day. Quilts in the
WCTU's signature colors of blue and white were
made in communities up and down the land, and
many of the graphic blue and white nineteenth-
century examples seen today were Union-
inspired. Another fervor of making quilts for
fund-raising took place early in the twentieth

century in aid of the Red Cross. The international
relief organization was founded in Switzerland
in 1859, and the American Association of the Red
Cross became a registered component in 1881.
The work of the US organization expanded
dramatically during World War I, and large
numbers of red and white quilts, many with
signatures, were made to raise money for the relief
efforts among the military and civilian
populations.

Dating techniques

Many quilts can be dated by the method used to
make the signatures permanent. Names on the
oldest quilts are usually worked in cross-stitch.
Stem stitch and chain stitch became popular later,

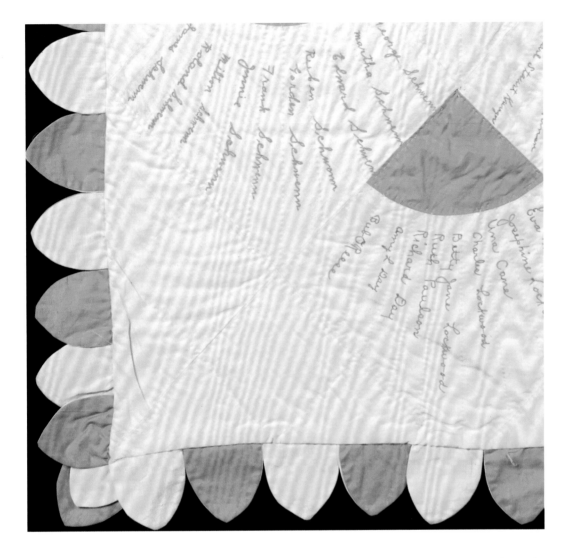

DETAIL

Fans Signature Quilt, page 62. Signature quilts were often a means to raise funds for the local church or to repair civic buildings.
Pieced and embroidered: orange on white.

ID 1979.233.1

and are found on quilts made between the end of the Civil War and the beginning of World War II, almost 100 years. Written signatures, dates, and pictures began to appear without embroidery in the 1830s, after the development of indelible inks that did not eat away the fabric on which it was used, in the way that earlier inks, which were made with iron or tannin, did. Many nineteenth-century examples retain their writing legibly, including poems or proverbs as well as the names and dates that were included.

Signatures can be found on quilts of all types. Many patchwork blocks have an area that lends itself to being used as a place to sign, and some of them are called simply "album" blocks. Bear's Paw, Turkey Tracks, and Courthouse Square are

all found as the basis for an album quilt. Quilts that appear to be wholecloth examples are often covered with signatures on a plain background. These usually comprise blocks that have been joined to make a coherent whole, which allowed the signers and embroiderers to work separately in order perhaps to finish a quilt quickly. Appliqué quilts were also widely worked, and there are many crazy quilts from the last quarter of the nineteenth century bearing numerous signatures.

Local groups, from churches and their support groups to charitable organizations set up to promote myriad causes in the community, still make signature quilts, which are then raffled or auctioned to raise money for the designated cause or presented as a gift to a worthy recipient.

SIGNATURE FANS

A HUGE VARIETY of Fans and Plates appear on American folk art quilts from the middle of the nineteenth century, but most are pieced from strips, often scraps, unlike the quilt shown here. The usual fan, often known as Grandmother's Fan, or called by its Victorian name, Fanny's Fan, has a quarter circle in one corner of a square block with blades radiating outward from the curve. The number of blades varies, and the shape at the top of the blades ranges from flat to pointed to curved. It can be set in myriad ways, square or on point, with all the blades pointing in the same direction or alternating to create a circular effect or curving rows, or with the corners facing each other to make wheels or butterfly shapes. Fan blocks are often separated with setting squares that provide space for elaborate quilting. Blades can be made from scraps, or from alternating colors; from checks or stripes. Fan quilts are found made from wool or cotton or silk.

Plates are best known in the Dresden Plate pattern, or a similar block known as Sunflower. The design has been used since the late eighteenth century, and was popular, like its companion fan pattern, throughout the nineteenth and into the twentieth century. Fans and Plates both appear frequently on Victorian crazy quilts made in silks and velvets and embellished with embroidery, as well as on sampler quilts from all eras. Patterns for both Grandmother's Fan and Dresden Plate were published in the early twentieth century, and feedsacks (see page 40) were widely used to make both designs during the Great Depression when money was scarce and the brightly colored printed fabric bags that held seed, animal feed, and dry kitchen ingredients were a great boon to thrifty farm wives across the country, who used them to make quilts and other household linens.

The thing that sets this late 1920's quilt apart from its sisters is the fact that the blades are quilted diagonally on the background fabric and then signed, so the only piecing that is needed is the applying of the orange quarter circle in the corner of each block. Ten signatures appear on each block inside the quilted blades—a total of 400 names—and each is embroidered with orange thread. The blocks are set on point side by side. A border on the sides and bottom edge of the quilt is made from pieced orange and white tabs, each attached individually with the colors alternating. In the two bottom corners a small tab has been laid on top of the larger one, again with the colors alternated. There are no tabs at the top edge, which would normally have been hidden by the bed's pillows.

The quilt was made for Pastor Calvin Martin Zenk (1882–1952) and his wife Emma (1884–1975) by members of the Immanuel United Church of Christ in the town of Dane, Wisconsin. A native of Wisconsin, Pastor Zenk began his career in the clergy in 1908 at Saint Thomas Church in Chicago, Illinois, and married Emma at about the same time. He held parishes in Sauk City, Wisconsin; Norwood, Ohio; and Madison, Wisconsin, before he retired in 1949, but was never the minister at Immanuel, so the reason he was given this elaborate and also highly personal quilt is not known.

FANS SIGNATURE QUILT
1925–1930

Maker(s) unknown; member of Immanuel United Church of Christ, Dane WI.
90 x 71 in.
(229 x 180 cm)

ID 1979.233.1

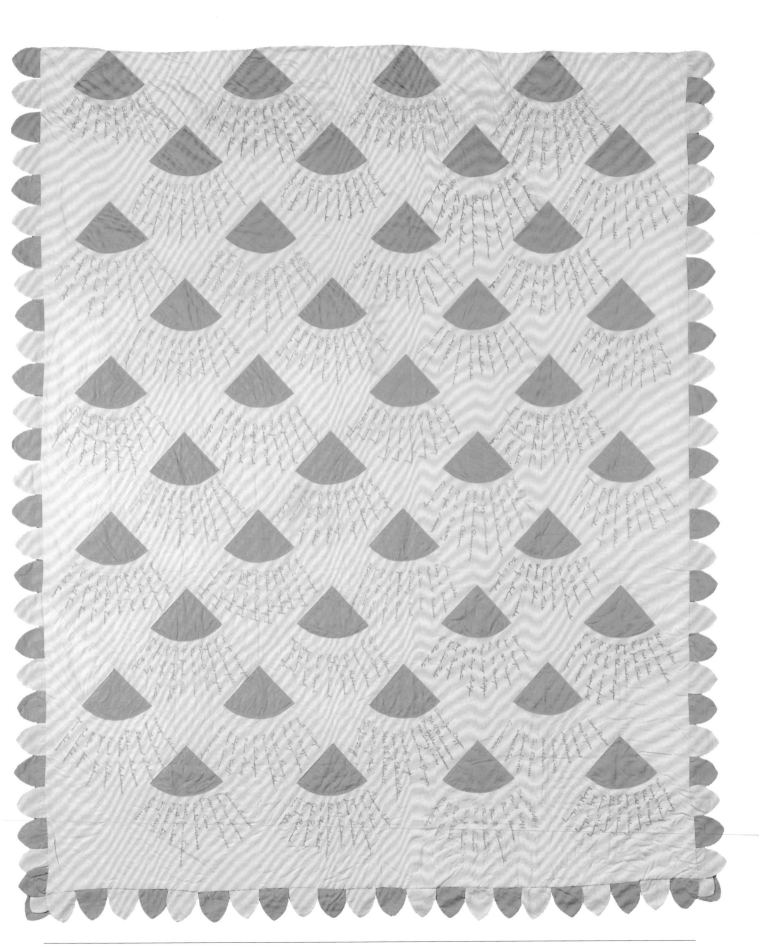

CHIMNEY SWEEP

CHIMNEY SWEEP
SIGNATURE QUILT
1849

Maker(s) unknown;
friends of Mary
Catherine McCool
Foster.
93¼ x 82 in.
(237 x 208 cm)

ID 1945.1340

Quilt names changed as people moved from place to place. A quilter might devise her own name for a block, perhaps to commemorate an event or even just to be different. Many block names were based around biblical themes or political events. Their origins are lost, but the names are still with us.

The name of the block in this quilt has even more variations than most. It has been used as a block on signature and friendship quilts since the early nineteenth century, and one of its earliest names is Album Patch. It is pieced, and it was perhaps to distinguish it from the appliquéd album quilts that were made from the mid-1800s that several other names began to be used. Chimney Sweep seems to have been the most widely used alternative, together with Courthouse Square (not to be confused with Courthouse Steps, see page 82, which is a variation of the Log Cabin pattern). Other variations include Friendship Chain and Christian Cross, but all are basically the same pattern of colored squares surrounding a cross of pale hue in the center, which can be made from five light-colored squares, or two squares and a rectangle of the same width and three times the length of the squares.

The central area was large enough to make an ideal place for writing signatures, dates, or messages, and the small size of the outer squares meant the pattern was easy to create using scraps, particularly beneficial if the quilt was being made—as often happened—from worn clothes or household linen connected to the recipient of the gift.

The names on the quilt shown here are written, like the date "1849" and the various sayings that are included, in ink, a popular method for signing friendship quilts. This quilt was given to Mary Catherine McCool Foster (1831–1909) at the time of her wedding. Born in Lewisburg, Pennsylvania, Mary Catherine and her eight siblings moved in 1840 when their parents relocated to northern Illinois, and she married Charles Stuart Foster (1819–1872), who was born in Maine but lived in Monroe, Wisconsin, in 1840. Of their seven children only three survived to adulthood, and one of them, Mary Stuart Foster, presented the quilt to the Wisconsin Historical Society. Mary Catherine moved to Madison in 1879 and died in 1909.

The red cotton fabrics used to make the border, the outer half-blocks that surround the piece, and the small corner squares in the sashing mean that the overall impression is of a "red" quilt, although yellow, green, brown, and pink all play their part in creating a lively look. Most of the blocks are fashioned from one printed or solid-colored fabric combined with the plain muslin background, but one block combines a red and yellow print with a plain red. The fussy cutting and careful arrangement of the green striped fabric indicate a quiltmaker of some experience and a well-developed sense of design. Setting the blocks on point makes the signed strips appear horizontal. The quilting is a simple cable on the sashing strips, while a series of squares quilted parallel to the edges of each block run counter to the seams and hold the batting securely in place.

RED AND WHITE CHEVRON

MAKING QUILTS from strips of fabric is perhaps one of the oldest methods used. Certainly it is one of the easiest, and there are numerous ways of putting strips together, giving an enormous range of designs, from a simple Rail Fence to a complex Pineapple Log Cabin, with patterns like strippy Chinese Coins (see page 78) or Modern Blocks (see page 80) in between. String-pieced quilts, created using strips of uneven widths, are a mainstay of African-American quiltmaking, with the vibrant improvisations that result being likened to jazz music. Geometric patterns, particularly Spider's Web, Four-Patch, and Nine-Patch, as well as many other well-known traditional block patterns, are cut from string-pieced units and found in great numbers. Log Cabin patterns are strip-pieced (see pages 78, 80 and 83), as are patterns based on rectangles like Brick Wall (see page 100).

The quilt shown here is pieced from interlocking rectangles and squares that have been offset to create a highly unusual chevron or zigzag design. It is a signature quilt that also falls into the category of fundraising quilt. Red and white were, together with blue and white, undoubtedly the most popular colors used by quiltmakers in the nineteenth century. The highly graphic effect created by using only red and white is found throughout the history of design, and once the colorfast red dye developed in the mid-1800s, called Turkey red (see page 19), became quite widely available, its use was immediately widespread.

The Willing Workers of Appleton, Wisconsin's, 4th Ward chose red and white to make this presentation quilt. Many Protestant churches in nineteenth-century America had a group of Willing Workers, who did sewing and quilting in aid of the church and its work. The 4th Ward Chapel in Appleton opened in 1889, an outpost of the First Congregational Church in the town, and it is thought that the red and white quilt was made to raise money for the chapel and its ministry.

Whatever its main purpose was, this quilt carries the signatures of 455 people, each of which has been written in ink on a white strip; and because most of the handwriting is similar, it is presumed that a small number of calligraphers with exceeding neat and legible handwriting have inscribed the names of members of the church and any others who paid a subscription. The central red area has been embroidered in white with the inscription "Presented to F. J. Harwood by Willing Workers of 4th Ward/1891" in a tight stem stitch.

Frank James Harwood (1855–1940) was born on Christmas Day in Crown Point, New York. He moved in 1874 to Ripon, Wisconsin, and then in 1876 to Appleton, where he founded Appleton Woolen Mills, which was one of a number of successful textile mills created to process wool in the area of the Fox River valley. He became a senior deacon and superintendent of the Sunday School at Appleton's First Congregational Church, serving between 1882 and 1922. As a prominent member of the congregation, he was selected to receive the quilt shown here once it was completed.

Each separate rectangle is outline quilted on the inside of the shape. The backing is muslin, and all of the edges are finished with a narrow red binding.

RED AND WHITE CHEVRON SIGNATURE QUILT 1891

Maker(s) unknown; members of Willing Workers, 4th Ward Chapel, Appleton WI. 85 X 70 in. (216 x 178 cm)

ID 1974.1.35

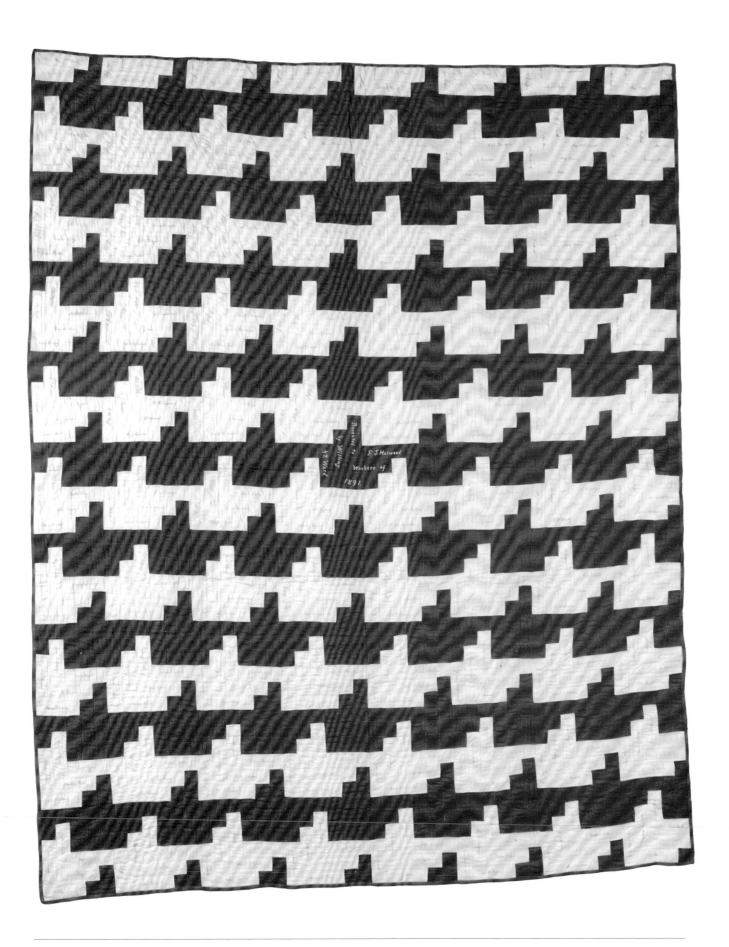

OAK LEAF

OAK LEAF
SIGNATURE QUILT
1846

Maker unknown.
102½ x 96 in.
(260 x 244 cm)

ID 1946.294

THE OAK LEAF has long been a favorite motif, and its use on quilts dates back to early appliquéd examples. Oak leaves on antique British quilts are thought to signify the naval traditions of the British Empire, since the ships of the Royal Navy that plied all the oceans of the world were made of oak. Their use in quilt design has been varied. The pattern of the quilt shown on these pages, based on four leaves joined at the base and applied to a plain background to make a square block, is one of the simplest. Similar patterns have a ring of cherries in the spaces between the leaves, while one of the oldest American folk art appliqué motifs usually has acorns at the base of the leaf that form a ring in the center of the block. This version is called Charter Oak, named, according to Dolores A. Hinson in *A Quilter's Companion* (1973), for the oak tree in which certain citizens of Connecticut took it upon themselves in 1687 to hide the charter issued to the colony by the British government, which had threatened to revoke the document.

The best known oak leaf block is probably Oak Leaf and Reel, in which a ring, or reel, surrounds a four-sided motif and has a leaf in each corner attached to the ring. The block, or a variation, appears on most Baltimore Album quilts. It was widely worked in the heyday of red and green appliqué quilts, in the latter half of the nineteenth century, a popularity made possible partly by the widespread use of the first colorfast red dye, called Turkey red (see page 19). Many of the most graphic surviving quilts from this period are red and white, and most are remarkable for the brightness of the color, even though it was laid down more than a century ago. A good number of red, green, and white examples still exist as well, but the green dye of the period was less successful than the red and has often faded dramatically. Called a "fugitive" color, it tended to lose its brilliance, and many green motifs on antique quilts now appear to be brown or tan as a result.

The forty-nine blocks on the quilt shown here, dated 1846, measure 12 inches (30 cm). Each block has four leaves that meet in a small central square, where the ink-lettered signatures occur, most decorated with a tiny drawing, though some of the motifs are blurred. The leaves are print fabrics, probably large scraps, with opposites matching each other in each block. The background is white cotton, and red is the predominant color, with a scattering of blue, green, and pink, and a fair amount of yellow. The mitered border, on three sides, is a gold, white, and green printed floral vine climbing a trellis. The leaves are outline quilted.

To many people, oak leaves traditionally symbolized long life, strength, and fertility, and they were widely used in wedding quilts as a way of wishing the couple a long and fruitful marriage. This quilt was probably one of these, made for Margaret Krips Miller (1823–1904) when she married John S. Miller, a Baptist minister, in Philadelphia, Pennsylvania, in 1847. The couple moved to Madison, Wisconsin, in 1880. According to the 1850 census records for Philadelphia County, Pennsylvania, the names include several members of the Krips family, and it is likely that many others included were related to the bride.

GEOMETRIC QUILTS

Many of the best known traditional quilt designs are geometric patterns. Some are based on simple one-patch shapes such as hexagons or diamonds; others are extremely complex and incorporate numerous shapes in different sizes to make a coherent whole. The most popular combinations among today's quiltmakers are those that can be rotary cut and speed-pieced, which means patterns that use squares or rectangles combined with right-angle triangles, but numerous other geometric figures can be found throughout the history of quiltmaking.

DETAIL

Modern Blocks, page 80. The colors in each block are carefully arranged to balance, but to give the overall impression that the block is either dark or light.
Pieced: multicolor strips.

ID 1975.132.6

Many of the patterns used to make traditional pieced, or patchwork, folk art quilts rely heavily on geometry. The qualities inherent in geometric principles are essential elements, together with the choice of colors, the juxtaposition of light and dark values, and the scale of fabric patterns, in creating a pleasing visual effect—which is of course what most quiltmakers strive for. The size of a block, and of the elements within the block, the width of borders and sashing, even the choice of shape are all geometric elements that need to be considered in the design of a quilt.

Quilts can be created by repeating a single shape—squares or rectangles, of course, and hexagons and diamonds are popular choices for these "one-patch" patterns—or by combining a number of different shapes, such as triangles, squares, and rectangles, into elaborate blocks that are joined to make an even more intricate overall design. These block quilts often result in secondary patterns that, depending on color placement and value, enhance the design and even become the element of the quilt with the most impact. If patchwork blocks are alternated with plain ones, they create a grid and give space for elaborate quilting motifs that would be lost if they were worked on the pieced blocks. Setting the blocks "on point" gives a diamond grid that provides a totally different visual experience. Quilts can be conjured from strips, narrow or wide, vertical or horizontal, even or skewed. All can be transformed into wonderfully lively and fascinating pieces of folk art.

Early quilts

The earliest quilts that found their way to the New World came mainly with British colonials who settled the east coast of North America in increasing numbers after the beginning of the eighteenth century. Their quilts were usually simple wholecloth and medallion quilts (see pages 30–41), and their layout generally followed

geometric rules of a sort. Attempts were usually made to design the size of the "frames" around the central shape, whether it was by using a different quilting motif on a wholecloth or a row of pieced blocks on a medallion, to balance in overall impact. Simple strippy quilts, with their vertical lengths of coordinating or contrasting fabrics, also used elements of balance and geometry to provide visually pleasing results. These settlers made quilts in their traditional ways, at first using and re-using fabrics imported from Britain. After independence the textile mills of New England geared up and produced much

DETAIL

Chinese Coins, page
78. Scraps of fabric
were carefully hoarded
and recycled into
wonderfully colorful
quilts.
Pieced: multicolor
strips, with black.

ID 1974.1.34

of the cloth required by the country, a great deal of it spun from cotton grown in the southern states and wool from American sheep.

By the time the middle of the United States—the area between the Appalachian Mountains and the Rockies—had evolved into settled communities and farms, making quilts from blocks had become a standard design approach. The fledgling US added huge territories during the first half of the 1800s, and land grants drew homesteaders to the areas in large numbers. These pioneers, many weeks of travel from the eastern seaboard with its cities and manufactured products, had few possessions with them and limited space to store what they did own. The climate could be harsh and unforgiving, with savagely hot summers and bitterly cold winters, and warm covers were a necessity for survival. Because new fabric, made in the textile mills of faraway New England, was difficult to obtain and expensive to purchase, scraps were hoarded and recycled. The block quilt existed before, but it came into its own with the homesteaders, who could make a block when they had time and a supply of scraps, and then set it aside until they had enough blocks to put together a quilt.

Quiltmaking, however, could not take precedence over all the other tasks that women oversaw. Planting, weeding, harvesting, and cooking food were part of a woman's work in rural societies. So were soapmaking, laundry and housework, childcare, and religious duties and education. Then there was spinning, weaving, mending, darning, and making all the clothes worn by the family. Quiltmaking was often a job that was relegated to the evening hours, when all the other tasks of the day had been completed. But quilts obviously provided an outlet for the innate creativity of many of these pioneer women, and surviving quilts are a testament to the ability of many of them to combine colors and create great beauty with only limited time and resources.

Quilting also provided a social outlet for many women, in towns and cities as well as in the countryside. The sewing and quilting bee have long been a staple of American life. Women got together to make contact and to quilt or sew. Many bees were large gatherings to which a farm wife could take her finished quilt tops, which were then quilted by a group of friends working around a quilting frame. Fabric scraps and quilt patterns, recipes and gossip could all be exchanged while quilts were finished. As life became more settled and prosperity increased as the nineteenth century progressed, bees were organized to promote causes or raise money for favorite charitable endeavors. They remained, however, the partly social occasions they had always been.

DETAIL

Honeycomb Quilt, page 84. The hexagon is one of the most versatile geometric shapes.
Pieced: multicolor prints with white.

ID 1971.163.1

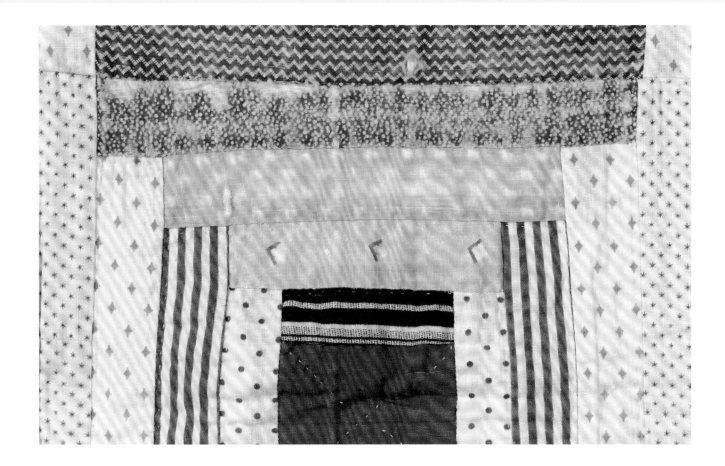

Geometric patterns

Patterns migrated with the settlers, and recognizable ones were given names that became standard designs, such as Log Cabin, Pinwheel, Shoofly, and any number of different star patterns. The designs may have been standard, but the number of variations for all of them defy imagination. The basic Log Cabin pattern combines strips of fabric around a center square, but depending on the order in which the strips are attached, the block can be called Courthouse Steps, or Pineapple, or Cabin in the Cotton. The center can be any shape, from triangular to random. Small squares or triangles can be placed in the corners of each row of strips to create secondary patterns in individual blocks that make tertiary patterns when they are combined. And the sets, or overall combination, of the blocks have their own names, such as Light and Dark, Sunshine and Shadow, Barn Raising, Straight Furrow, and Streak of Lightning.

Sometimes a pattern has a name unique to a particular community, as in Gee's Bend, Alabama, where several generations of talented quiltmakers have dubbed any Log Cabin-type pattern as "Housetop."

Some names were fanciful—Drunkard's Path, Tangled Garter; others described forms from nature—Oak Leaf and Reel—or everyday objects—Weathervane. Hexagon patterns are called Grandmother's Flower Garden, probably a 1930's invention, or Honeycomb, or they can be combined into pictorial images like baskets. Diamonds make Tumbling Blocks or Baby Blocks, and are used in many Star patterns, which also change names depending on location. The elaborate Star of Bethlehem became Lone Star when it reached Texas at about the time of that territory's short life as an independent country, and was called Star of the East in other places. All have in common their origins in the principles of geometry.

DETAIL

Courthouse Steps, page 82. This traditional block is arranged with the light and dark strips on opposite sides of the central shape, which is sometimes rectangular. Pieced: red, brown, green, black and multi-color prints.

ID 1968.577.17

OLD MAID'S RAMBLE

THE USE OF diagonal lines is a principle of design that works almost every time. Triangles and diamonds appear in all aspects of art and design because their slant draws the eye to areas that are important in the artist or designer's mind. Diagonal shapes also create a lively feel taking the eye in several directions at once.

The simplest triangle is created by slicing a square or rectangle in half diagonally. This "triangle square" or "right-angle triangle" forms the basis for countless patchwork blocks, and makes sewing easier because it ideally has two sides that are on the straight of grain, with only one bias edge. All other triangles have at least two bias edges—an isosceles triangle, for example, where only one side can be on the straight—and many, such as 60-degree, or equilateral, triangles, have three bias sides. True diamonds, not squares turned on point, can have two straight sides, but the other two must by definition be on the bias.

Many of the patterns using non-right-angle triangles and diamonds have traditionally been worked using a method called English paper piecing. Shapes are cut from paper to the finished size of the patch and basted to a fabric patch cut slightly larger. The paper template keeps the edges of the fabric shape rigid while patches are joined. This technique, which is also widely used to make hexagon quilts, is worked by hand and requires many hours of labor. Some short-cut methods have been devised by clever quilters, but many people prefer to use patterns that use triangle squares.

Two sizes of triangle squares have been used to make the blocks with their diagonal pattern in the quilt top shown here. The pattern is called Old Maid's Ramble by Barbara Brackman and Maggie Malone, both respected late twentieth-century quilt historians. It is very similar to Lady of the Lake, a pattern documented in two early twentieth-century histories. In *Old Patchwork Quilts* (page 76) published in 1929, Ruth E. Finley shows a quilt called Lady of the Lake, made in Vermont before 1820. She surmises that the pattern was named after the poem written by Sir Walter Scott in 1810 and says that it has never experienced a name change. Later in the book, she shows a different block, called Indian Trail, and says that it takes her award for the pattern that has changed its name the most. Among those names is Old Maid's Ramble. Carrie A. Hall and Rose Kretsinger, in their 1935 *The Romance of the Patchwork Quilt in America* (page 100–101), make the same claim that the pattern has "never been known by any other name," but one of the blocks they illustrate is identical to the Old Maid's Ramble in our quilt.

Made between 1890 and 1910, this Old Maid's Ramble top uses printed cotton fabrics for all the shapes except the light sides of the small triangle squares, which are cream muslin. The piecing has been done by hand except on some sections of the triple border, which is made from the blue print and cream print used to make the large triangle squares.

OLD MAID'S RAMBLE
1890–1910

Maker unknown.
94 x 81 in.
(239 x 206 cm)

ID 1971.183.4

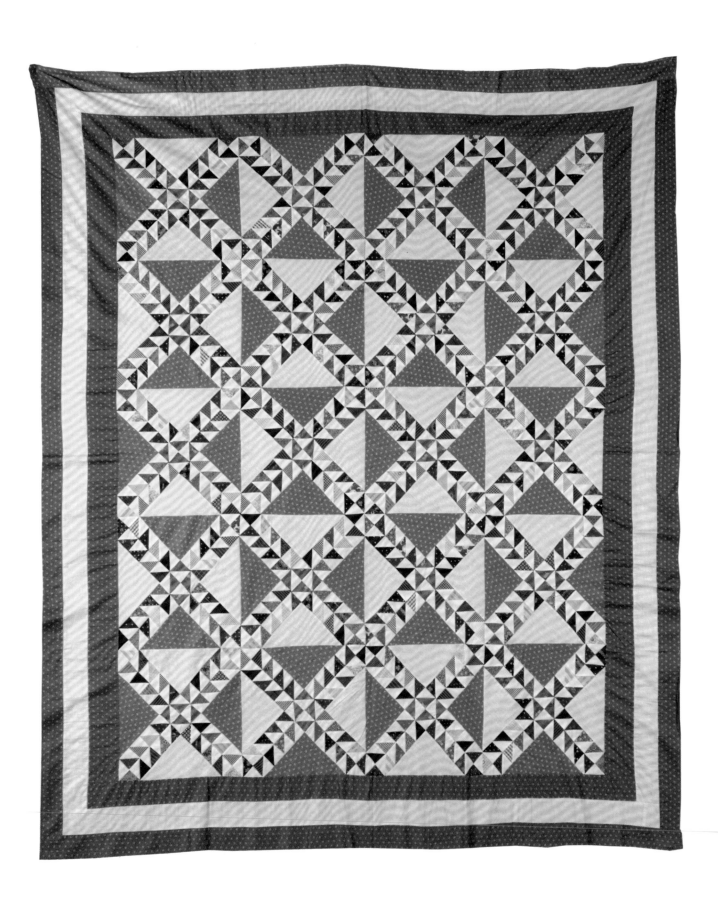

CHINESE COINS

GEOMETRIC QUILTS

CHINESE COINS
1875–1900

Maker unknown.
68¼ x 61 in.
(173 x 155 cm)

ID 1974.1.34

QUILTS MADE from narrow strips of fabric have been made for many decades. Called "strippy quilts," or strippies, or strip quilts, they are generally highly graphic, and often appeal to modern aesthetics. The fact that, in their most basic form, they are relatively simple to construct means they have been popular with quiltmakers on both sides of the Atlantic at least since the mid-nineteenth century.

At their simplest, they are made from strips, usually arranged vertically, of two alternating highly contrasting fabrics. Some of the finest British examples come from County Durham and Northumberland in the northeast of England. Made in large numbers from mid-century, they were often elaborately quilted within each strip and had a plain backing that could be used as a wholecloth quilt (see pages 30–41) when turned over. Some examples contain several different fabrics, but great care was usually taken to make sure the strips coordinate well. Strips were generally the same width, but in some examples there are wide and narrow strips akin to sashing.

The tradition of these "Durham strippies" was taken up enthusiastically by American quiltmakers. They were often a way to show off the highly valued chintz fabrics imported before the Civil War. Colorful chintz, which had originated in India and was a major British cloth manufacturers' export, could be combined with plain muslin to stretch the expensive import to make good use of its beauty. American versions soon became more elaborate than the plainer but more heavily quilted British quilts. Alternate strips were sewn as traditional block patterns, not as sometimes happens on British examples, when strips are often pieced to make up the length if the quiltmaker ran short of cloth. Four-Patch and Nine-Patch blocks were widely used, allowing the quiltmaker to dip into her scrap basket, while other designs such as stars are also found. Bands of Flying Geese (see page 94) were also popular.

Two distinct groups of American quiltmakers adapted the strippy idea into their own traditions. African American quiltmakers often make quilts from strips, which in some areas are called "Lazy Gal." These are less rigid, more fluid in shape. The strips are not always straight, and the quilting tends to be utilitarian.

The Amish, particularly in Pennsylvania, began creating their version, which they call "Bars," in the nineteenth century. Bars quilts are usually closer to Durham strippies than to their American cousins. They use a limited color palette, often dark, rich colors, and the quilting tends to be of high quality. But whereas British strippies have no borders or binding, Amish Bars have both, so the area where the bars are becomes the center of an adaptation of a medallion quilt as well.

The quilt shown here is pieced in a design that was also popular in the Amish tradition called Chinese Coins, or Roman Coins, or Roman Stripe. Made in the last quarter of the nineteenth century, it is constructed from strips of silk and velvet dressmaking scraps sewn together into seven 7-inch (17.5-cm) wide bands that are alternated and bordered with narrow dark blue velvet strips. The backing is a striped silk taffeta in purple and gray with a bias border mitered at the corners.

MODERN BLOCKS

SEWING STRIPS of fabric together to make a larger piece of cloth is perhaps the easiest way to piece a quilt. Humankind's early ancestors made clothing and shelter by joining strips of leather or fur or, later, cloth. Primitive bedcovers may have been made in the same way.

Strips don't have to be the same width or length. They don't even have to have straight edges, and the resulting string-pieced fabrics are lively and visually interesting. Many African American quilts are string-pieced from strips of varying width to create exciting quilts with an improvisational nature that have been called fabric jazz.

More often, though, strips are used in American quilts to make patterns that have a geometric regularity. Many traditional block patterns are today made from strips that are cut with a rotary cutter to a certain width, sewn into lengths, and cut again into pieced strips that are joined to make blocks of a particular design. Other methods have been devised by modern quiltmakers, such as one that involves sewing strips in lengths, making a tube which is cut into strips across the piecing, then taking out on seam in each pieced strip to facilitate color placement. Strips are used to make blocks for Log Cabin (see page 83), Rail Fence, Roman Stripe, and Chinese Coins (see page 78) quilts, as well as for pieced borders such as Piano Keys.

The Seminole tribe of Florida work with strips of bright solid-colored fabrics that are joined lengthwise, cut into different strips either widthwise or at an angle, then resewn into elaborate geometric bands of fabric. The resulting cloth is then used to make garments and bags on a commercial basis, bringing income into the tribal coffers.

Successful quilts rely on contrasts: of color, of value, of texture, of balance, of shapes. The quilt shown here combines all these qualities. It is constructed from blocks made of five strips of equal width. Most of the blocks contain three different fabrics—all silk and velvet dressmaking scraps—arranged carefully to balance within the block itself but give an overall impression of being either a light block or a dark one. These units are set on point to create alternating vertical rows of light and dark, and the strips alternate with darks pointing in one direction and the lights running the other way to give a satisfying rhythm to the piece. The outer edges of the blocks inside the borders are finished with matching triangles of strips, also carefully positioned to match.

There are two borders; the inner one is made of black velvet in an unusual octagonal shape. Its edges are embroidered with an elaborate and closely worked floral garland on the inside and a double zigzag with long stitches similar to a tuft of grass or an ear of wheat on the outer side. The outer border is pieced from narrow alternating triangles that are scalloped on the outside similar to an ice cream cone design. The scallops are embroidered with a tight buttonhole stitch.

MODERN BLOCKS
1875–1890

Maker unknown.
63 x 56 in.
(160 x 142 cm)

ID 1975.132.6

COURTHOUSE STEPS

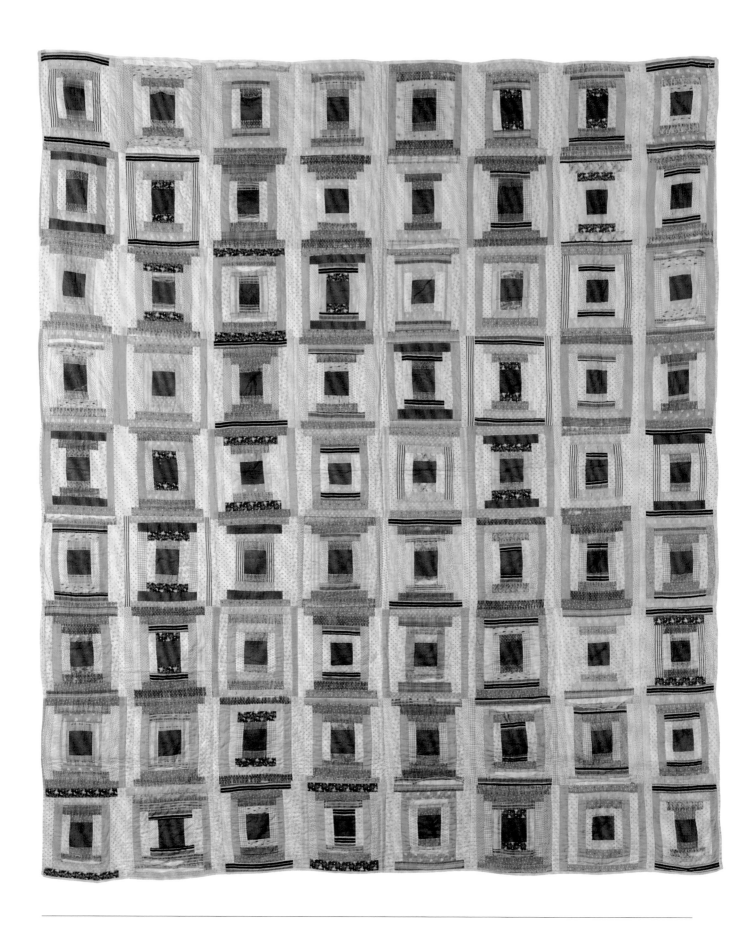

GEOMETRIC QUILTS

LOG CABIN is the pattern that most people associate with American patchwork quilts. Its construction is simple, its use of fabric frugal, and its variations endless. It is thought that the name Log Cabin gained common parlance during Abraham Lincoln's presidential campaign in 1859–1860, when his humble roots in a log cabin in Illinois were used both to endorse him and to malign his suitability to lead the nation, but it has been used by quiltmakers on both sides of the Atlantic for more than two centuries. The earliest American examples that have been found date from the 1860s, but there are older surviving quilts in Britain. Most areas of the British Isles have quiltmaking traditions, and Log Cabin patterns are found in them all, from Scotland and Ireland, to both the west and north of England, and even the Isle of Man, where the pattern was called Rooftop.

Log Cabin has a number of named variations, such as Courthouse Steps, White House Steps, Cabin in the Cotton, and Pineapple. The basic Log Cabin block is created by stitching strips of fabric in a particular order around a central square so that two adjoining sides of the block are light and two are dark. This gives a diagonal rhythm to the blocks, which are set side by side without sashing to make the top.

The way the blocks are joined creates an overall effect, called a secondary pattern. Many of these designs also have names. Light and Dark (or Sunshine and Shadow) has the light sides of four blocks juxtaposed, then four darks, etc., which creates larger areas of light and dark, which can either appear as squares or as diamonds, depending on whether the blocks are set square or on point. Barn Raising creates bands of light and dark that represent walls laid on the ground before being "raised" to make a barn, an essential structure in rural life. Straight Furrow alternates blocks to make stripes of light and dark running diagonally through the quilt, while in Streak of Lightning the layout creates zigzags. There are also literally countless variations on all of these named patterns.

The quilt shown here is a lively example of the Courthouse Steps block in a utilitarian bedcover. It contains a highly traditional feature of Log Cabin: the center squares are red, thought to represent the fire or hearth at the heart of every home while the strips are laid around it like house logs. Most Log Cabin quilts from the nineteenth century have this characteristic, though some have yellow centers, and others are black, thought to represent a judge in his robes. Courthouse Steps is arranged with the light and dark strips on opposite sides of the central shape, which is often rectangular. In this 1890's example, the darks are mainly shades of brown with a distribution of greens, reds, and blacks, while the light sides are small-scale printed shirting fabrics. The maker has used a number of red prints on the light sides, which has the effect of squaring off the blocks in an unusual way. The batting is cotton, the backing plain muslin, and the quilt is bound with a cotton print.

COURTHOUSE STEPS
1885–1895

Maker unknown.
76 x 72 in.
(193 x 183 cm)

ID 1968.577.17

HONEYCOMB QUILT

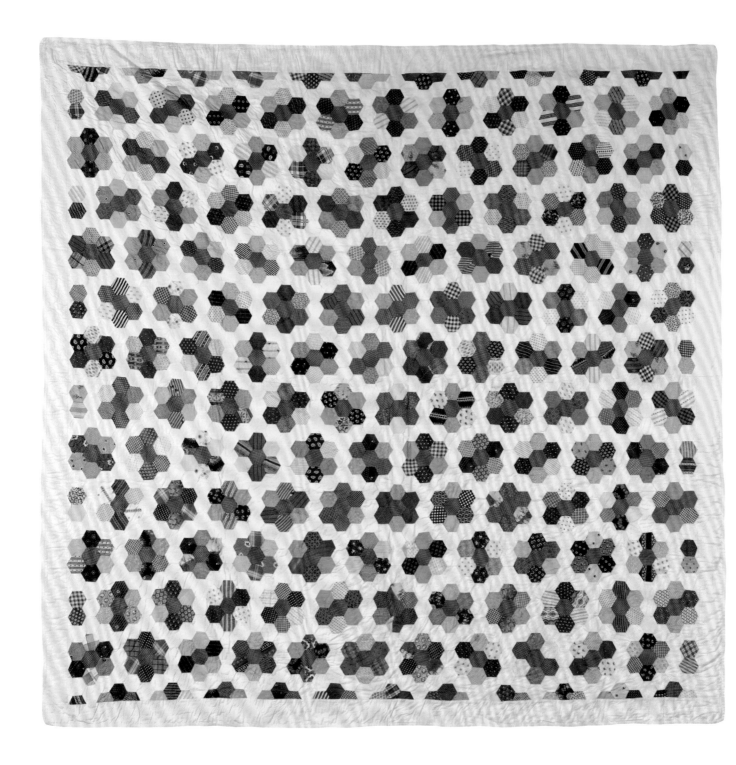

GEOMETRIC QUILTS

HONEYCOMB QUILT
1880–1900

Made by Olive
Amanda Kendall
Crippen (1842–1925).
81 x 78 in.
(206 x 198 cm)

ID 1971.163.1

MOSAIC PATTERNS are found in design in virtually every culture around the world. The term "mosaic" comes from the fact that these interlocking arrangements of shapes were widely found in Mediterranean societies, especially the Roman Empire, as tiles arranged on floors and walls, but the intricate patterns are part of the language of design.

The hexagon is one of the most versatile of all the geometric shapes. Its six sides can be joined to others of its kind, or it can be combined with 60-degree triangles or equilateral triangles in most intriguing ways. Hexagon quilts are made from wool, silk, cotton, and synthetics. The traditional method for stitching the sides, only two of which can ever be on the straight of grain, is to cut paper shapes of the finished size and baste each fabric piece, cut slightly larger, to a paper template. When all the shapes have been joined, the papers are removed so the quilt can be layered and quilted. Numerous tops have been found with many of the basted papers—often letters or newspapers—intact, which has been enormously helpful in dating them. Although methods have been devised for rotary-cutting the shapes and piecing hexagons by machine, most hexagon quilts are still made by hand.

Hexagon quilts have been made in America since the eighteenth century. The best known type of hexagon quilt is undoubtedly Grandmother's Flower Garden, in which six hexagons are joined in a ring around a seventh to make a rosette that is then outlined with a background row or two of hexagons. The rosettes are generally made from bright fabrics with a white or cream background, and the final row is often green. The name was applied to the pattern in the late nineteenth and early twentieth centuries, but the basic pattern has long been part of the quiltmaker's lexicon since the ideas and construction methods were almost certainly brought with the early English colonists. They would have been familiar with the design, which has been found in tile mosaics since Roman times. Hexagons were often used to outline the center on medallion quilts and then to make entire quilts called Honeycomb or Mosaic.

Different color placement creates totally new patterns, from stripes of color to Trip Around the World arrangements that can make diamond or hexagonal secondary patterns. If a hexagon is added to two opposite sides of a rosette, a diamond shape is created that can then be used in the same way as ordinary rosettes, with astonishing results. Pictorial patterns, such as flower bouquets and baskets, are also often made from hexagons.

The quilt shown here goes by the old-fashioned name of Honeycomb. It was made by Olive Amanda Kendall Crippen (1842–1925), born in Palmyra, Maine. By the time of the 1860 census, she was living with her parents in Michigan. She married David A. Crippen (1824–1892) in 1873, and they lived in Alpena, Wisconsin.

The fabrics are scraps of cotton prints in a variety of browns, reds, double pinks, and greens with some blue scattered throughout. There are a number of plaids, checks, and stripes included, and the same brown geometric print appears as the center for all the rosettes. The background rows that separate the individual rosettes are muslin, and a similar fabric has been used for the 3-inch wide borders and for the backing. It is simply quilted in parallel lines and filled with wool batting.

SMALL QUILTS

Small quilts have a special place in the history of quiltmaking.

Most quilts measuring under thirty-six inches (90 cm) square

were made for babies and toddlers, while even smaller examples

were made as doll quilts. Both were generally intended to be

used and loved and, unlike their full-size counterparts, fewer of

these tiny wonders have survived the many hours of covering

small children or their favorite dollies and the laundering that

would have been needed to keep them clean. Where they have

been handed down to subsequent generations, they offer a

wonderful glimpse at quiltmaking on a small scale.

THE STORY OF SMALL QUILTS

DETAIL

Irish Chain Doll Quilt, page 92. This pattern is made up of small squares so is a good way to use up small scraps of fabric. Pieced: red and white.

ID 1950.5920

SMALL QUILTS include those made for babies and children, as well as doll quilts. These little treasures are fascinating for their history, and offer quiltmakers the opportunity to try out patterns on a small scale. Small quilts are often miniature quilts, technically scaled-down versions of full-sized ones, but they can simply be small in overall size. Crib quilts are usually made with love as gifts for a specific baby.

Childhood as we view it today is a recent phenomenon. The doting on babies and children that we experience in the twenty-first century didn't begin to happen in Western societies until the 1800s, when children began to be viewed as small versions of adults and were expected to behave themselves accordingly. Previously children were considered useful and to some extent expendable, sent to work in dangerous or even life-threatening situations at shockingly young ages. Life was cheap, and many youngsters never made it to adulthood.

A change in attitude happened gradually; child labor laws were first enacted in Britain in the mid-1800s and education became more widespread and accessible to a greater percentage of the population than ever before. The number of children working declined and schooling increased, and respect for the innocent child became more widespread. Material goods intended for the use and enjoyment of the young began to be created, small quilts among them. Quiltmaking was a widely practiced activity at the time, and it is probably not unrelated that myriad small quilts were made in the nineteenth century. They were sometimes created from one or more extra blocks left from a larger project, and small quilts were sometimes made from part of a damaged or worn quilt by cutting them down and re-binding. The best are scaled-down versions of full-sized quilts, some of which are made from tiny patches, beautifully planned and executed. Strippy quilt patterns (see page 72) were popular and widely used on small quilts.

Doll quilts

Among other benefits, the making of small quilts, especially those for dolls and their beds or cradles, provided an excellent way for children to learn stitching skills, in much the same way that embroidered samplers were used to teach young girls to sew in earlier centuries. While samplers also helped the young stitchers master their alphabets and numbers, quiltmaking could be used to teach aesthetic skills of color and design as well as figuring out the mathmatical aspects involved. After making quilts for their dolls, girls could move on to making small quilts for baby brothers and sisters before tackling larger-scale projects which would have been part of their training for adulthood, at a time when the woman's role in society generally was to look after the home and the people in it.

Many of the doll quilts created by children in the nineteenth and early twentieth centuries were made by hand. Skills were being learned and there are usually mistakes, especially in sizing blocks. As sewing machines became more affordable, small quilts were often machine quilted by an adult, saving time in busy households, but many were hand quilted by the small piecer. Antique examples of elaborate or finely worked doll quilts exist—most of these were likely to have been made by adults as special gifts. Child-made doll quilts were generally simple designs based on four-patch and nine-patch square or rectangular patterns made from small scraps probably left over from a mother's sewing basket. Very few appliqué examples have been found. The charm of child-made doll quilts lies in their naivety and spontaneity. They display an exuberant innocence that often comes from an untrained or inexperienced maker trying out ideas while learning new skills.

Cradle quilts

Cradle quilts were listed in household accounts books as early as the late Middle Ages in England,

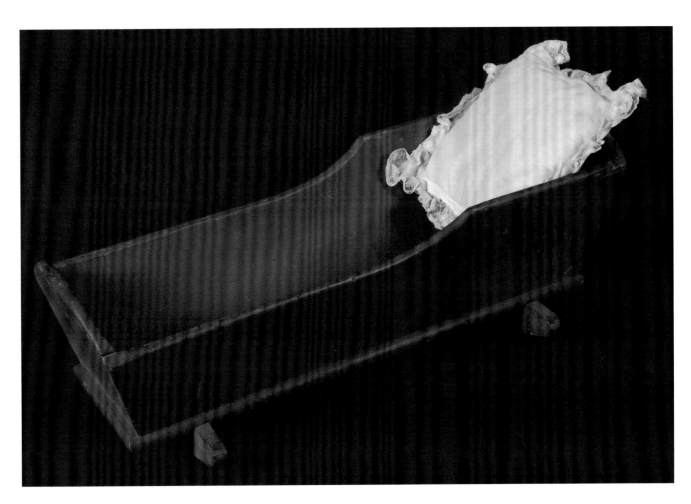

ABOVE

An orange-painted pine doll cradle, thought to have been handmade by a Wisconsin lumberjack, was given to Margaret La Mieux Bruce on her fourth birthday in 1873.

ID 1945.353

DETAIL

Four-patch Doll Quilt, page 109. This quilt was donated with the cradle shown above. Pieced: multicolor prints.

ID 1945.1551

and the tradition was transported to the colonies along with so much else. In the nineteenth century, most girls put together a "bottom drawer" or "hope chest" in which they kept items that would be part of their trousseau or dowry when they married. Items of clothing, particularly lingerie, and household linens, including a dozen quilt tops, were traditionally among the contents made by the hopeful young lady. Once an engagement was announced, a quilting bee would be scheduled, and friends and family members would meet to quilt the tops that would provide warm bedcovers for the bride and groom. Crib quilts were not usually included in the hope chest, but were generally made specifically for each baby as he or she arrived. Surviving cradle quilts made especially for newborn babies are usually worked as miniature wholecloth quilts from baby-soft fabrics and are generally finely stitched with fairly elaborate quilting patterns, but they usually have no other decoration such as appliqué or embroidery.

By the nineteenth century, crib quilts were usually about 36 inches (90 cm) square, and the best are scaled-down versions of larger patterns. Because they were subjected to frequent laundering and heavy use, many that have survived show their age. By the early twentieth century, crib quilts with childhood themes had become popular. There are many examples of pictorial quilts, usually appliquéd, that were made from patterns published in the newspapers and magazines of the day, as well as redwork transfers (see pages 50–51) of nursery themes and traditional block patchwork patterns, often in pastel hues, scaled down to reflect the overall size of the piece. Kits for crib quilts were widely available as well.

Cradles and dolls

Doll quilts that have found their way into museum collections are sometimes donated with the doll for which they were made, and occasionally the bed or cradle on which they lay accompany the donation as well. The small quilts in this chapter reflect the important aspects of these little gems, which are fairly rare and therefore highly desirable and cherished.

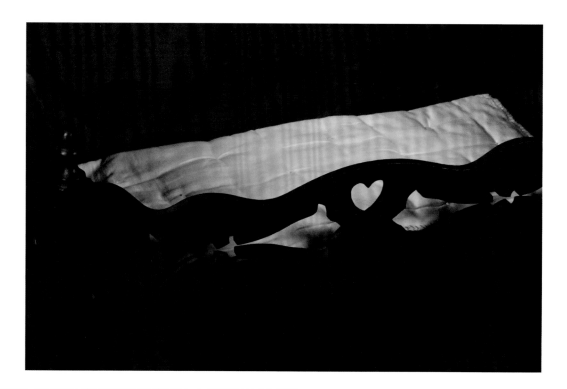

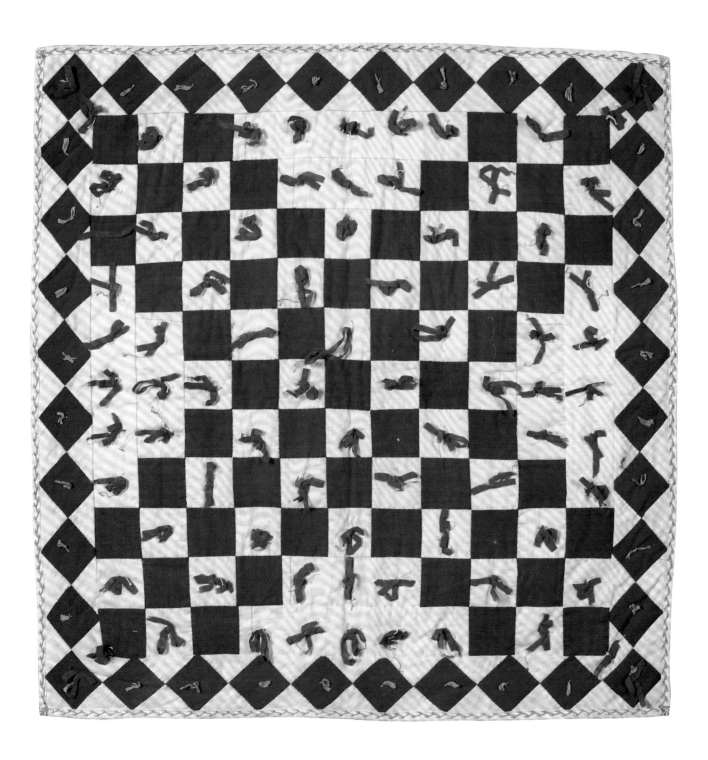

IRISH CHAIN

IRISH CHAIN DOLL
QUILT
1900–1925

Maker unknown.
21½ x 21½ in.
(55 x 55 cm)

ID 1950.5920

THE IRISH CHAIN pattern, composed mainly of small squares, has been a favorite of folk art quiltmakers for decades. Two different blocks are usually required to make the design, which depends on strong color contrasts for maximum impact. Many of the most striking examples are two colors only. Red and white (or cream) is the most popular color choice, particularly in nineteenth-century quilts made after the colorfast dye known as Turkey red (see page 19) became commercially available. Dark blue and white examples are also widely seen, but other colors, including prints, were used. It works well using scraps, and many makers no doubt found the pattern a good way to use up small pieces from their scrap bag.

There are three variations of the Irish Chain pattern: Single, Double, and Triple. They differ in the number of small squares making the chain. The simplest version of single Irish Chain is made from double nine-patch blocks, and the chain appears as a series of single squares. Double Irish Chain starts with a five-patch block arranged in a checkerboard pattern of 25 small squares. When plain strips with corner squares are added to these pieced blocks and to a similar number of plain ones, they can all be joined to make a quilt top with the chain three squares wide. Triple Irish Chain requires many seams to make the five-square-wide chain, but the results can be stunning.

If Irish Chain blocks are set square, the pattern of the chain will be diagonal. Turned on point, the blocks form a horizontal and vertical grid. Plain setting squares lend themselves to decoration, and examples with beautiful appliqué or elaborate quilting, including trapunto, can be seen. Borders on historical examples tend to be simple or nonexistent.

No one knows why the pattern is called Irish Chain. There is no evidence that the pattern originated in Ireland, and in some areas of Ireland, the pattern is actually called American Chain. Examples have been found in the British Isles and in North America that date from the colonial days of the late eighteenth century, and the pattern is still popular today. It was widely made by Amish quilters using their traditional solid colors.

The Irish Chain doll quilt shown here has the charm that these small pieces often display. It is a Triple Irish Chain made from $1^1/_2$-inch (4 cm) red and white cotton squares. The chain and the four white triangular areas in the center of each side of the X are all set square, while the outside edges are made as a pieced border using squares of red set on point and separated by white triangles on either side. The quilt is tied in different ways: the white squares, and the four red corner squares, with quarter-inch-wide (6 mm) red silk ribbons, each about 6 inches (15 cm) long. The red squares have white embroidery floss ties. The backing is white muslin, and the back-to-front binding is held in place with feather stitching worked with pink embroidery floss, while the same floss is also used to tie the red border squares.

FLYING GEESE CRIB QUILT

FLYING GEESE is a traditional pattern that was used in Britain on early bed quilts. It is found on eighteen-century medallion, or frame, quilts (see page 72), usually as one or more of the "frames" around the central panel, the "medallion," of these early quilts. Such quilts are made up of a series of borders surrounding the center, which was frequently a piece of highly prized and expensive chintz that the maker wished to show off. Some of the borders are simply strips of fabric, often chintz as well, while the majority of the "frames" are pieced strips. Many of the best-known traditional blocks that are so much a part of American folk art have their origins in these pieced patterns, such as simple triangle squares, pinwheels and windmills, and many star patterns. Four-patch and nine-patch borders abound, as do designs created from diamonds and triangles. Corner blocks are usually different from those used to make the framing strips, and the width of the borders varies, usually increasing from the center outward but often with narrow borders of equal width between the widening frames.

Flying Geese units can be made in pairs and formed into blocks. All the "geese" can "fly" in the same direction, or they can alternate individually or in groups. However, the most frequently seen use of Flying Geese is in strips such as the ones on the quilt shown here. It is found on strip quilts (see page 72) from many regions and quilting traditions, from the traditional strippies of County Durham and Northumberland in the northeast of England, to Bars quilts from the Amish areas of the United States, to the improvisational work of African American quilters throughout the South. The vertical strips that make up quilts of this type are an ideal format for Flying Geese, which is also called Wild Geese Flying or Wild Goose Chase.

Flying Geese units are made from one large right-angle triangle, usually in a color, with two smaller right-angle triangles arranged one on each short side of the large triangle to create a rectangle. They can be cut as individual shapes, or foundation-pieced on paper patterns, and various speed-piecing methods have been devised by clever quiltmakers. The smaller triangles are usually light-colored to act as a background, and when Flying Geese are used in strip quilts such as this one, using the same fabric for the alternating plain (unpieced) strips gives a good-sized area for background quilting.

This Flying Geese crib quilt is made from triangles of a striped fabric. Its narrow stripes are green, yellow, and blue, with green as the dominant color, and white cotton background triangles and alternate strips. The same white cotton has been used for the backing, while a narrow binding of a double brown printed cotton fabric finishes the edges. The quilting, which covers the entire quilt, is simple diagonal crosshatching.

The condition of the quilt indicates that it was little used, or well cared for, or both, for it is in good shape for its age.

FLYING GEESE CRIB
QUILT
1875–1878

Maker unknown.
44 x 41 in.
(112 x 104 cm)

ID 1975.292

SUNBURST CRIB QUILT

THE PATTERN known as Sunburst is composed entirely of 60-degree diamonds sewn together in a way that creates an explosion of color. The design begins with an eight-pointed star in one color and continues in rings of contrasting color all the way to the edges of the quilt.

Sunburst is related to other star patterns such as Star of Bethlehem, which is also called Lone Star, and a variation called Broken Star. All these patterns have traditionally been constructed using the English paper piecing method, in which a template of the diamond shape is cut to the finished size from paper and a slightly larger fabric shape is basted to the template. These basted pieces are then sewn together using a whipstitch or small blanket stitch. When the top is finished, the papers and basting are removed and the quilt is layered, quilted, and bound. This method is also used to make Tumbling Blocks or Baby Blocks quilts, as well as hexagon designs and some patterns involving triangles.

The names for all these star patterns are interchanged, but Sunburst is usually defined by its rings of color that go to the edges, while Lone Star and Star of Bethlehem create large-scale stars with setting squares at the corners and setting triangles in between each point. Broken Star is even more complex, with a smaller star in the center surrounded by setting squares, with rings of colored diamonds beyond. The setting squares create a secondary eight-point star, usually in a solid-colored fabric, and the outer ring of diamonds makes a sixteen-point star, which are in turn surrounded by setting squares and triangles. The solid areas created by the squares and triangles give a wonderful blank canvas just perfect for elaborate quilting. The setting squares in particular on all three star patterns are sometimes pieced as well, often with smaller versions of the main star motif.

This Sunburst quilt is a crib quilt, perhaps made for a very special baby, considering the amount of work that would have been involved. It is pieced primarily from cotton prints, predominantly reds, yellows, and shades of brown with a scattering of blues throughout. Stripes and checks have been used to great effect and contribute to the lively overall feel of the quilt. Many Sunburst quilts use the same fabric to make each ring, but in this example the anonymous quiltmaker has alternated both color and value in the rings, making it a feast for the eye and an interesting sampler of late nineteenth-century fabrics. In the first ring she has used a pale blue solid fabric and made the points from pale yellow that harmonize with the brown and white stripe of the central star. The next ring is darker in value and composed from a dark red and a dark blue print with beige points. The following rings alternate in value, with the fabrics in carefully balanced pairs, and the outer points of each ring different from the other fabrics in that ring. The backing is brown and blue check, while the binding is a blue and white floral print. The quilting follows the shapes of the diamond pieces.

SUNBURST CRIB QUILT
c. 1899

Maker unknown.
38 x 36½ in.
(97 x 93 cm)

ID 1949.876

WREATH AND DOVE

TRADITIONAL appliqué uses many stylized forms from nature, from trees and flowers to birds, insects, and other animals to fruit and the occasional vegetable. Early American settlers brought ideas and designs from their homelands to the colonies. Many of the motifs found on colonial- and federal-era quilts had been handed down through generations, including patterns that are found on early English textiles from the days of the Tudor monarchs and their successors, beginning with King James I. The natural forms on these embroideries, tapestries, and bed hangings were adapted into patterns that appear on quilts from the eighteenth century onward.

In the nineteenth century American quiltmakers began to make quilts formed from blocks. These units were easy to work on, and could be stored more conveniently than a large quilt, until enough blocks had been completed to make an entire top. Traditional patterns were reworked and redesigned to fit into a square, usually from about 12–15 inches (30–37.5 cm), and many of the simpler appliqué designs were made more elaborate by the addition of more leaves, or buds, or motifs of various kinds. Large numbers of mid-century appliqué quilts were made as four-block quilts, with an elaborate motif replicated four times on large background squares which were then joined to make a full-size quilt. Sometimes these blocks are sashed, and many four-block quilts have equally elaborate borders that on the best examples are a variation of the main motifs of the blocks. They were often designed in a way that left plenty of space to add quilting. The size of the blocks—approximately eighteen inches (45 cm)—could, with a border or two added, also make a single-block doll or crib quilt.

This charming naive appliquéd doll quilt is a quintessential work of American folk art. Perhaps it was made as a practice block for a larger quilt, or by a child learning how to sew. Made during the American Civil War, it is possible that—bearing in mind that the battles were affecting the entire country—the bird represents a dove of peace, but these birds were widely used in many art forms. The wreath is a variation of the President's Wreath appliqué block that was enormously popular in the middle of the nineteenth century, and the quilt is made in the red and green on white color combination that was widely used at the time.

The centers of the open rose flowers are also typical of the era. These touches are sometimes worked in reverse appliqué as here, where the centers have been cut and the edges of the shape turned under and sewn down with blindstitch. The centers are sometimes a different color, most often yellow. To work them in reverse appliqué, a small piece of fabric was worked into a cut-out area on the appliquéd fabric and sewn in place. Some flower centers were separate circles that were applied in the usual way, while in other examples they were worked as embroidered satin stitch or French knots. The quadruple border is made from three-quarter-inch (18 mm) strips of different red and green fabrics, and the red used on the innermost border has also been used to bind the quilt, which is backed with simple plain white cotton.

WREATH AND DOVE
DOLL QUILT
1850–1870

Maker unknown.
23½ x 23½ in.
(60 x 60 cm)

ID 1945.1258

BRICK WALL

BRICK WALL DOLL
QUILT
1870–1880

Maker unknown.
29 x 26 in.
(74 x 66 cm)

ID 1956.1123

CLOTH MADE from strips of fabric may be the earliest form of patchwork, though the biodegradable nature and ephemeral qualities of textiles makes it impossible to know when humans first started to patch in strips. Quilts made from strips of fabric are generally referred to as "strip quilts" or "strip-pieced quilts." The category includes Log Cabin in all its variations and also encompasses String-pieced quilts, which are made from strips of uneven width. String piecing has been practiced by African American quiltmakers since slave days, and the results are generally as exciting to the eye as jazz music is to the ear. Nineteenth-century quiltmakers used long strips left over from dressmaking projects, which were generally quite narrow and usually not even in width, by sewing them to a foundation backing and then cutting the resulting fabric into pieces for making traditional blocks like Spider's Web or various star patterns, while in the twentieth and twenty-first centuries, designs like Bargello, formed from strips cut from larger pieced fabrics and then stitched with the colors offset from row to row to create wavelike patterns, have become popular.

The Brick Wall pattern, like many other patterns made from rectangles or squares, can be assembled by stitching the patches into long strips end to end, as opposed to the vertical rows found in designs like the Chinese Coins quilt found on page 78, and then joining the strips as rows. The scrappy quality of many Brick Wall quilts shows the frugality for which quiltmakers are renowned —what better way to make use of small scraps than to turn them into a funky piece of fabric that then becomes usable. The rectangles used to make a Brick Wall quilt should of course be offset row by row if the piece is to look like a real wall constructed from building bricks, but part of the charm of many Brick Wall quilts is the random nature of the finished product.

The Brick Wall doll quilt shown here contains an interesting selection of mid-nineteenth century calico prints as well as woven geometric patterns, both checks and stripes. The predominant color is red, which always pops out, and there is a scattering of browns, pinks, beiges, and blues, including one small patch of dark blue in contrast with the pale blues found elsewhere. The maker's scrap basket was certainly eclectic, but the fabrics tend to blend with each other within each color range, and several are used only once or twice. The backing is a red and white striped cotton that has also been used to make the binding. The entire quilt is machine pieced, and the machine quilting is worked in diagonal lines. It was made at a time when home sewing machines were becoming widespread, and this small quilt could have been a practice piece for someone learning to use the newfangled mechanism. Or it could have been cut down from a larger quilt, which often happened, especially as the backing and binding appear to be of a newer vintage than the fabrics in the quilt itself.

TEXAS STAR CRIB QUILT

THE SYMBOL represented by a star is one of hope and light. Most of the world's religions use stars in their iconography, and the flags of many nations carry one or more stars. So it is perhaps not surprising that star patterns are found more often in quilts than any other design category, and they are used in many folk art quilts. Not only are they visually pleasing and in many cases easy to draft as patterns, they are also incredibly versatile, and the variation that can be found in star patterns is virtually endless. Simple stars create wonderful geometric designs and can be made more complex by the choice of fabrics, such as checks and stripes. More complicated patterns, such as the Sunburst quilt on page 96, can be works of art that withstand the test of time. Patchwork stars generally have even numbers of points, usually either six or eight, but the complex patterns such as Mariner's Compass can have many more. Six-point stars are formed from diamonds or triangles, and can be transformed into many configurations from simple hexagon stars to the highly complex pattern known as Seven Sisters, in which six stars made from 60-degree diamonds surround a seventh central star of a different color. Each star is separated from its neighbors by setting diamonds and the block forms a large hexagon block. Eight-point stars can also be created from 45-degree diamonds or triangle squares (see page 76), the simplest of which is known as LeMoyne Star, or Lemon Star.

The pattern called Texas Star is a variation of an eight-point star. Eight points on a star design such as this make it easy to create, since the points are all right-angle triangles in a nine-patch formation. There are at least a dozen named star patterns formed in a similar way, from Variable Star and Ohio Star to several Braced Stars, North Star, and Twin Stars. The form of all these patterns is basically the same, but the arrangement of the central area, and the choice of color and value, creates different configurations that have their own names.

The crib quilt shown here was made in 1850 by Marietta Brooks Smith Merrick when she was six years old. Born in 1844, she donated the quilt to the Wisconsin Historical Society in Madison, Wisconsin, in 1923. She was the daughter of a dyer in Greeneville, Connecticut, and was educated at the Norwich (Connecticut) Free Academy and Norton Female Seminary. In 1866 she married George Byron Merrick (1841–1931) in Washington DC. The couple moved to New York City in 1867, and then to Wisconsin in 1875. They lived first in River Falls and moved to Madison in 1885. They had one daughter, Winona (born 1869), but since the quilt is not finished, we must assume that neither mother nor daughter ever used it.

The quilt consists or eighteen pieced star blocks made from solid-colored and patterned cotton fabrics, some printed and some woven in geometric patterns, either checks or stripes. They are set on point and separated with setting squares and triangles made from a brown and green striped taffeta fabric. The unfinished edges are not bound, and the piece is not quilted, but a white cotton backing is attached.

TEXAS STAR CRIB
QUILT
1850

Made by Marietta
Brooks Smith Merrick
(1844–1937).
48 x 36 in.
(122 x 91 cm)

ID 1946.308b

DOLL QUILTS

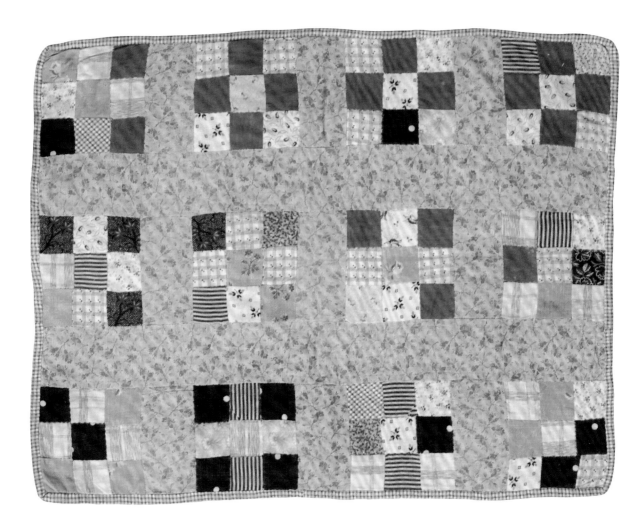

NINE-PATCH DOLL QUILT WITH SASHING
1877

Maker Lorinda Clark Couch (1842–?), Greenbush, Wisconsin; present to Jane "Jennie" Goessling Hammitt (1881–1965)
17½ x 13½ in. (44 x 34 cm)

ID 1946.320

COTTON REEL DOLL QUILT
1900

Maker unknown.
19¾ x 15¼ in. (50 x 39 cm)

ID 1971.23.10

THERE ARE beautiful doll quilts, and there are rough-and-ready doll quilts. There are simple doll quilts and elaborate ones. They can be pieced or appliquéd, quilted or tied, but one thing almost all doll quilts have in common is the fact that they have been used and loved. Perhaps that is why relatively few have survived, why they are treasured by collectors, and why even the most workaday examples sometimes end up in museums.

Because antique doll quilts were often made in a hurry, or by a child learning the art and craft of stitching, they can be full of mistakes. Some doll quilts were almost certainly cut down from larger, worn quilts and re-backed and rebound to get a little more use out of valuable fabric. Botched stitches, uneven quilting, pieces cut off at strange angles, and unusual color choices are all part of their charm. The six quilts on the following pages are all pieced, and they also share the feel of pieces made quickly to be used and enjoyed. Five of these examples are based on squares and are arranged as one-patch, or four-patch, or nine-patch patterns.

The first quilt shown here, an unquilted nine-patch with sashing, is a true scrap quilt. The sashing is brown and blue, the binding a red check. The backing is a coarse brown and white check, and there is no batting. The quilt was a Christmas present to Jane "Jennie" Goessling Hammitt (c.1881–1965), an early women's rights activist, in 1886 from the maker, Lorinda Clark Couch (1842–??). Both lived in or near Greenbush, Wisconsin.

The Cotton Reel, or Hourglass, quilt has twelve quarter-square triangle blocks made of men's tie

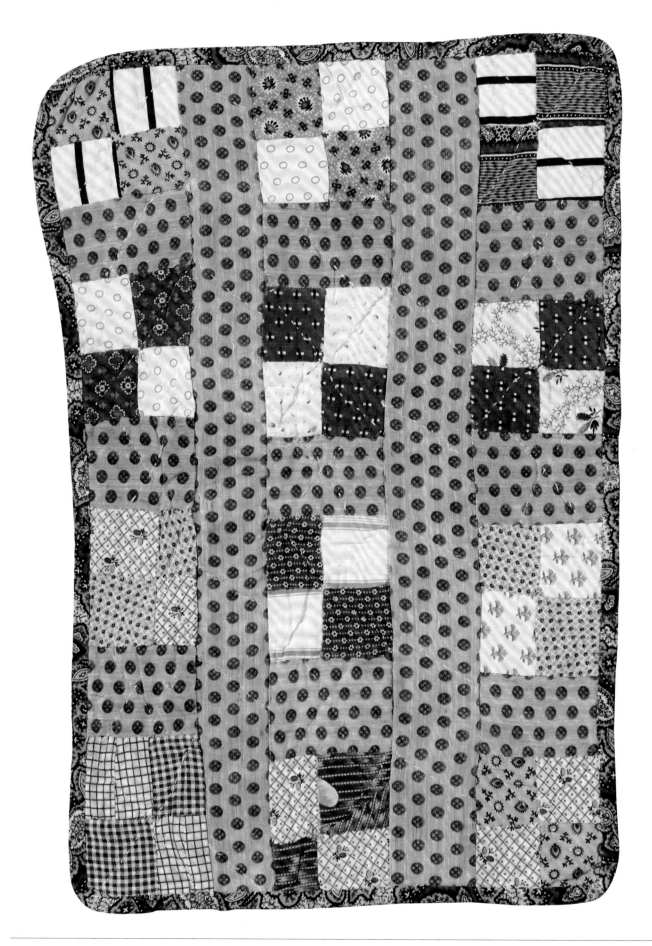

silk. There are stripes, solids, checks, and woven patterns in an alternating light and dark configuration. The backing is polished cotton, and it is bound edges to middle. There is no quilting.

In the third quilt, a sashed four-patch, brown predominates. Each block has either brown or beige patches, and the sashing is a roller-printed geometric. Even the backing is brown, and brown tones predominate in the paisley binding. The one-patch quilt with its central cross could have been a block left over from another project to which other squares were added. The printed cotton fabrics are still bright and the squares alternate between lights and darker shades. Browns predominate, but pinks, blues, red, and the green check around the center give the piece vitality. Both the backing and binding are the same brown-and-white floral print. It is machine quilted in vertical rows through the center of the squares with two horizontal rows, one in the center and one through the bottom row. Both these quilts were donations, given with an antique doll's cradle, to the Wisconsin State Historical Society.

The fifth quilt on page 108 is made of squares as a one-patch; the patches are dress silks. The back is also silk, pieced from three different fabrics, two of which have also been used to make the side borders, pieced from two 1 in. (2.5 cm) strips on one side and a 2 in. (5 cm) border on the other. The quilt came into the collection with the doll pictured on page 86.

FOUR-PATCH DOLL QUILT WITH SASHING
1870

Maker unknown.
16½ x 10½ in.
(42 x 27 cm)

ID 1946.965

ONE-PATCH DOLL QUILT WITH CENTRAL CROSS
1870

Maker unknown.
18 x 14 in. (46 x 16 cm)

ID 1946.966

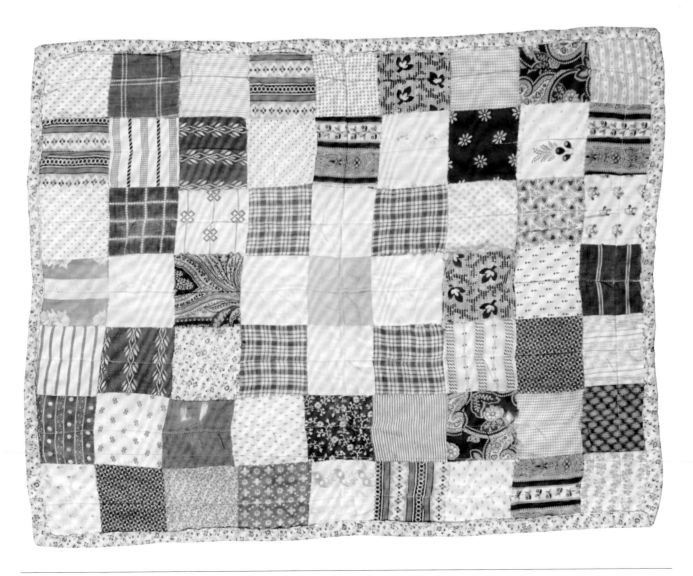

ONE-PATCH DOLL
QUILT WITH SIDE
BORDERS
1875–1900

Maker unknown.
22 x 16½ in.
(56 x 42 cm)

ID 1947.1253

FOUR-PATCH DOLL
QUILT

1875–1900

Probably made by
Margaret La Mieux
Bruce (c. 1869–?).
18¾ x 12½ in.
(45 x 32 cm)

ID 1945.1551

The simple four-patch blocks in the final quilt are set edge to edge. The printed cottons, primarily pinks and browns with blues, greens, and one yellow, are somewhat faded, and two squares have shattered, showing the cotton batting. Backed in cream muslin and quilted in a crosshatch along the diagonal of each patch, this quilt was also donated with a doll's cradle, shown on page 89.

THE WORKBOOK

We have selected six quilts, one from each chapter, and reproduced a block with step-by-step instructions. Two are pieced blocks. One is turned-edge hand applique. Two involve embroidery as embellishment, and one is trapunto quilting. We have tried to choose patterns that are unusual but at the same time introduce ideas and techniques that you may not have tried before.

In addition, the basic techniques used to make the projects are outlined, and we provide general instructions for making each of the quilts featured in the book, with cross-references to the techniques involved.

Happy quilting!

TOOLS AND EQUIPMENT

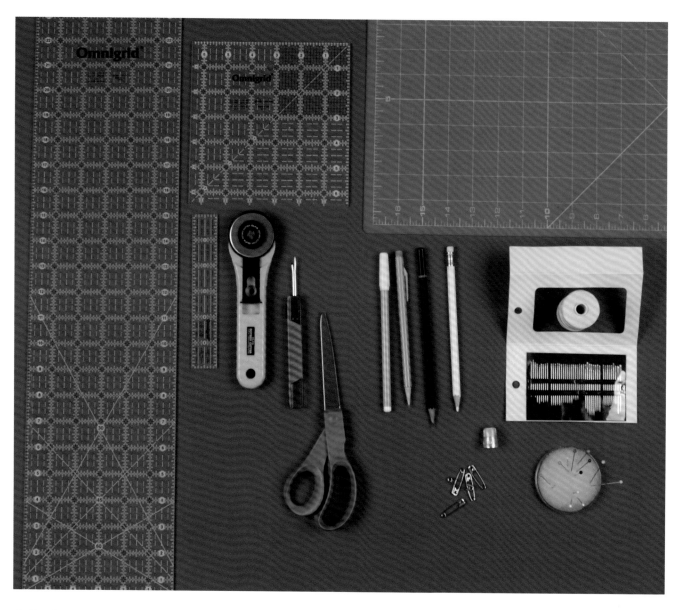

Quiltmaking doesn't require a great deal of specialized equipment. Most of the basic equipment is standard to any sewing basket, but there are a number of tools that have been developed that make the tasks involved quicker, often easier, and therefore more fun. Chief among these are the rotary cutting equipment pictured here: the cutter, which is available in several sizes and configurations; the ruler, or rulers, of which there are numerous variations, many with very specific uses; and the self-healing mat, which protects blade and work surface. There is also a vast selection of markers, each of which has its own characteristics, from water-soluble and air-soluble to permanent, erasable pencil, and various colors for working on light or dark fabrics.

Left to right:

Top: 24 x 6 in. (30 x 15 cm) rotary ruler, 6½ in. (16.5 cm) square rotary ruler, self-healing mat

Middle: 6 x 1 in. (15 x 2.5 cm) rotary ruler, rotary cutter, seam ripper, fabric scissors, water-soluble blue pen, lead pencil, erasable pencil, white pencil, thread, needle selection

Bottom: Safety pins for basting, thimble, pincushion with various pins.

BASIC TECHNIQUES

A comprehensive explanation of all the techniques used in patchwork, appliqué and quilting could—and does—fill several entire books, but the following pages outline the basic techniques that are used for the quilts in this book. For further explanation of quilting terms, see the glossary on pages 138–139.

JOINING FABRIC PIECES

Piecing means joining fabric shapes. The standard seam allowance used in quiltmaking is ¼ in. (6 mm) and a special quarter-inch, or patchwork, foot is available for modern sewing machines. Fabric shapes should be cut to the finished size plus ¼ in. (6 mm) allowance all around.

Joining pieces by hand

When patchwork shapes are to be joined by hand, the stitching line must be marked on the wrong side of the fabric. Line up two pieces and sew using a small running stitch along the marked lines, adding each piece in turn.

Joining pieces by machine

There is no need to mark the stitching line for most machine piecing. Cut strips or shapes carefully along the straight of grain and line up the edges of the pieces to be joined. Sew with right sides together using a quarter-inch foot to make a ¼ in. (6 mm) seam.

Chain-piecing is a quick method of joining several units without breaking the thread. Place piles of adjoining pieces at hand and feed them through the machine one after the other without lifting the foot or breaking the thread. Once they have all been pieced, cut the short threads that hold them together and press each unit.

A quick method for making triangle squares, which are used in many quilt designs, is shown on pages 116 and 120. To create a particular size of triangle square, add ½ in. (12 mm) to the finished size of a unit.

To join pieced units, press all seams to one side, alternating the direction from one piece to the next. Align the seams and line up the edges to be sewn. Take a ¼ in. (6 mm) seam. The rows should match precisely at each intersection between pieces.

To join blocks to make a quilt top, square up each block to the same size and join the blocks in rows, then join the rows.

Piecing on a foundation

Pieces can be fused to a foundation backing as in the Silk Ribbons quilt on pages 48–49. The raw edges then need to be secured with hand or machine embroidery.

In the method known as "stitch and flip" pieces of fabric are applied to the foundation fabric. The first piece is placed right side up on the foundation, usually starting in the center. The second piece is applied right side down with one edge lined up with an edge of the first piece. "Flip" the second piece to the right side and repeat with the third piece. Cover the entire foundation backing in this way, then trim the edges to square up the block.

English paper piecing

Many one-patch quilts, especially hexagons, diamonds, and clamshells, are made using the technique known as English paper piecing.

Cut paper templates to the finished size and fabric shapes with a generous ¼ in. (6 mm) seam allowance all around. Pin a paper to the wrong side of each fabric shape. Then fold the seam allowance over the edges of the paper and baste them in place, keeping the knots on the right side of the shapes to make it easier to remove the papers later.

Place two adjoining patches right sides together and make sure the corners are level. Blanket stitch or whipstitch along the exact edges, taking care not to stitch through the backing papers. Add adjoining patches in turn until the top is complete, then remove the backing papers.

APPLIQUÉ

Appliqué is the process of applying fabric pieces to a background fabric to create a design, either by hand or by machine.

Hand Appliqué

The traditional method of working this is called turned-edge appliqué. Cut out the shape in fabric, making it slightly larger all around than final size, and pin it to the background fabric. Turn under a tiny seam allowance all around with the point of the needle as you stitch the shape to the background fabric with small slipstitches.

Reverse appliqué

In this technique, several layers of fabric are basted together behind the top main fabric—the layers can be the same size as the top piece, or basted behind sections. The shape is marked on the top fabric and then cut away ¼ in. (6 mm) inside the marked line to expose the second layer beneath. The edges of the top fabric are turned under and slipstitched in place. The technique can be repeated on areas of the second layer to reveal the third layer and so on.

Machine appliqué

Appliqué shapes can also be fixed to a background fabric using machine stitching. Shapes for machine appliqué do not need a seam allowance so can be cut to size, before being fixed to the background fabric using pins, basting, basting spray or fusible webbing. Stitch around the shape with the machine, using zigzag stitch or any of the outline machine embroidery stitches.

EMBROIDERY

Embroidery is often used to embellish quilts and although any embroidery stitch can be used, here are a few of the most common.

Feather stitch

This is one of the basic embroidery stitches. It is worked downwards, making V-shaped stitches that alternate from side to side to create a feathery line.

Backstitch and Stem Stitch

Backstich is a row of small, evenly-spaced hand stitches, in which the needle enters the fabric at the end of the previous stitch so the stitch on the face of the fabric run end to

end, while on the reverse they overlap. It is used to create outlines or the effect of drawn lines. Stem stick is very similar, except the stitches on the face overlap, while on the reverse there is a neat row of backstitch.

Blanket stitch

Usually used as a border stitch to finish off raw edges, blanket stitch can also be used as a decorative feature. The needle goes into the fabric at an even distance from the edge

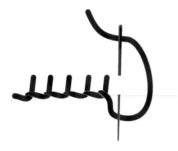

each time, coming out on the edge, and the thread is carried round the point of the needle at each stitch. Blanket stitch is worked with the vertical stitches set apart from each other, with buttonhole stitch they are set right next to each other.

Star stitch

An embroidery star formed by making an upright cross topped with a cross stitch, with all the arms of equal length. It is used to fill areas, either in rows, scattered randomly or arranged in a regular grid.

Chain stitch

This embroidery stitch is commonly used to create lines. It originated in India and Persia, although there it was worked with a fine hook called an ari instead of a needle. The needle goes back into the fabric right

next to where it emerged, then out again a small stitch away; wrap the thread around the needle point then pull the needle through to create a small oval stitch. Repeat to create a chain of overlapping oval stitches.

Herringbone stitch

This is worked from left to right, in a series of diagonal stitches up and down, crossing slightly at top and bottom.

Fly stitch

A simple embroidery stitch that is also a basic part of many other stitches. Draw two parallel lines and work a stitch across them, bringing the point of the needle up again in the center to catch the loop of thread and pull it down into a V shape.

FINISHING A QUILT

To finish your quilt you will need to join any individual blocks, adding sashing and borders if desired, then add backing and perhaps binding.

Adding sashing

Sashing consists of strips of fabric, which can be plain or pieced, that are used to separate and emphasize the pattern in quilt blocks. Usually vertical and horizontal, sashing strips can also run diagonally.

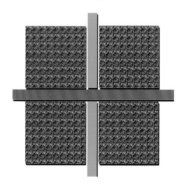

1 Sash blocks in rows using strips the length of the measurement of the block, with longer strips used to join the rows together.
.

Adding a border

Most quilts look best with a border to provide a frame around the basic design. Often a narrow inner border separates the main quilt from a wider outer border. There are three main methods of applying borders.

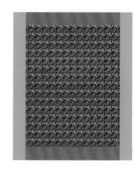

1 TOP AND TAIL: Add straight borders to the top and bottom edges of the quilt. Then add side borders to each long edge.

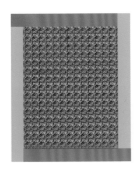

2 ROUND AND ROUND: Start on any edge 3–4 in. (7.5–10 cm) down from the top right-hand corner. Let the strip overhang the top edge of the quilt by the width of the border strip. Add the second, third, and fourth strips, working clockwise. To finish, sew from the point where you started stitching the first strip back to the top of the quilt.

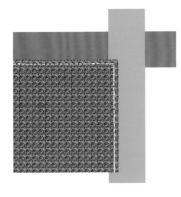

3 MITERED CORNERS: Cut strips and add twice the width of the border plus seam allowances. Sew the strip to the quilt with a ¼ in. (6 mm) seam and stop ¼ in. (6 mm) from the corner at both ends of the strip. Add each border strip in the same way.

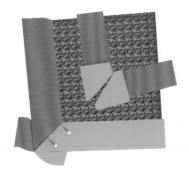

Fold back each strip to a 45-degree angle and press, then pin the fold.

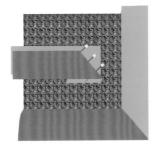

Re-pin on the wrong side at right angles to the fold and stitch from the inner corner to the edge.

Batting and backing

Batting is the padded material in the middle of a quilt that provides warmth and softness. It can be polyester, cotton, a blend of the two, wool, or silk. In the past blankets or even old, worn quilts were used. Backing is the fabric on the back of the quilt. It can be plain or pieced.

To layer a quilt, lay the backing wrong side up on a flat surface and lay the batting on top. Both layers should be cut slightly larger than the quilt top, since they tend to draw up when quilted. Lay the quilt top right side up on the batting. All three layers should be stretched taut and edges should be level. Baste the layers together with fairly large, easy to remove stitches or safety pins. The quilt is now ready to be quilted.

Binding

There are several basic methods for binding the edges of a quilt.

1 SINGLE BINDING: Join 1-in. (2.5-cm) wide strips of fabric to make a piece long enough to go all the way around the quilt. Press the strip with wrong sides facing along the lengthwise center, then press one side edge into the middle. With a ¼ in. (6 mm) seam allowance, sew the binding, with the unpressed edge right side down, to the edge of the quilt top. Turn the binding strip to the back of the quilt and pin and slipstitch it in place along the pressed fold.

2 DOUBLE BINDING: Cut a binding strip 2 in. (5 cm) wide and press to the center along the length. Sew the raw edges of the strip to the right side of the quilt top and turn the binding to the back. Slipstitch in place along the pressed fold. Double binding is obviously stronger than single.

3 SELF-BINDING, OR BACK TO FRONT: Cut the backing larger than the quilt top. How large you cut it depends on how wide you want your binding to be. Center the top, right side down, and the batting on the wrong side of the backing and even up all four sides. Press ¼ in. (6 mm) to the wrong side of the backing along all four edges. Turn the backing to the front of the quilt and pin along the pressed fold. Slipstitch by hand or machine topstitch along the fold.

4 EDGES TO MIDDLE: Cut the batting ½ in. (12 mm) smaller than the quilt top and backing all around. Fold the edges of the backing over the batting and pin in place. Turn the edges of the quilt top to the inside and re-pin through all layers. Topstitch a double row through all layers, first ½ in. (12 mm) from the finished edge of the quilt and then ¼ in. (6 mm) in from that.

TYING

Tying a quilt to hold the layers together is fairly quick and easy to do. Use cotton embroidery floss or pearl cotton, yarn, ribbon, string, or strong thread, and a needle with an eye large enough to take the chosen thread but which will go through the layers without difficulty. The knots are usually made on the top of the quilt, but some people prefer to hide them on the back.

Take the needle through the layers and take a small stitch, bringing the needle back to the working surface. Tie a square knot and then another.

You can either cut the thread and move to the next tying point, or you can take another stitch 3–4 in. (7.5–10 cm) away and tie a double square knot by taking the thread over and then under the length of thread that connects the two stitches. Continue taking similarly spaced stitches until the quilt has been tied at 3–4 in. 7.5–10 cm) intervals. Cut the connecting threads and trim the ends to the desired length.

BASKET OF FLOWERS

Basket patterns abound in quiltmaking, and this machine-pieced version is one of the most charming. It also works well made from scraps.

MATERIALS FOR ONE BLOCK
White cotton fabric
Blue cotton fabric
Rotary cutter, ruler, and mat

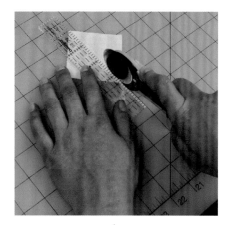

1 Make ten blue and white triangle squares by cutting a strip of each color 2⅜ in. (6 cm) wide by about 13 in. (32.5 cm) long. Mark off 2⅜ in. (6 cm) squares on the wrong side of the white strip and mark one diagonal in each square, alternating the line direction. Stitch ¼ in. (6 mm) from the line along the diagonal on both sides in each square. Cut the squares apart and then cut along the diagonal lines to make the triangle squares. Press the seam toward the dark side (see also page 124).

2 Cut two white 2⅜ in. (6 cm) squares. Cut them in half along the diagonal to make four triangles (you need three per block). Join them to three of the blue and white triangle squares made in Step 1 as shown in the diagram.

3 Cut a blue 5⅜ in. (13.5 cm) square and cut it in half along the diagonal (you need one triangle per block). Add it to the pieced square from Step 2 as shown in the diagram.

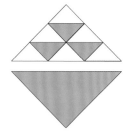

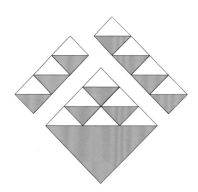

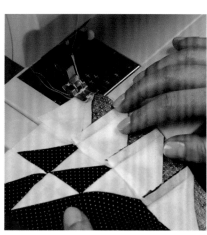

4 From the remaining blue and white triangle squares, make two strips, one with four squares and one with three squares as shown in the diagram above. Be sure to arrange the darks and lights as shown.

5 Join the strip of three to one side of the pieced square, then join the strip of four to the adjacent side as shown in the diagram.

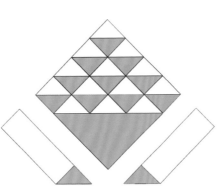

6 Cut two 2 x 5 in. (2.5 x 5 cm) white rectangles and one 2⅜ in. (6 cm) blue square. Cut the blue square in half along the diagonal. Add one of the resulting triangles to one end of each white rectangle. Be sure to make a right-hand and a left-hand version as shown in the diagram above.

7 Add one strip to each side of the pieced square with the small blue triangles at the tip of the large blue triangle as shown.

8 Cut a white 3⅜ in. (8.5 cm) triangle and add it to the bottom of the "basket" as shown to make a square block.

TRAPUNTO WHOLECLOTH

The template for this stylized cornucopia and several other motifs from the Trapunto quilt featured on pages 36–37 can be found on pages 134 and 136. Because it shows both corded and stuffed quilting, it is a good block to work first.

MATERIALS FOR ONE BLOCK
11 in. (27.5 cm) square of cotton background fabric
11 in. (27.5 cm) square of cheesecloth for backing
Washout marker
Basting thread and sewing needle
Quilting thread and needle
Cording wool and bodkin or tapestry needle
Fiberfill stuffing

1 Cut an 11 in. (27.5 cm) square of background fabric and one of backing. Here we have used a fine grade of cheesecloth (butter muslin). Trace the motif on the background fabric with a washout marker.

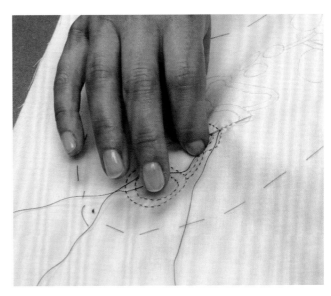

2 Baste the background to the backing well outside the marked motif. Using a running stitch, outline the motif. We have used a contrasting thread for clarity, but traditional trapunto is usually stitched in the same color as the background fabric. When all the outline stitching has been worked, wash out the marked lines and leave the block to dry completely.

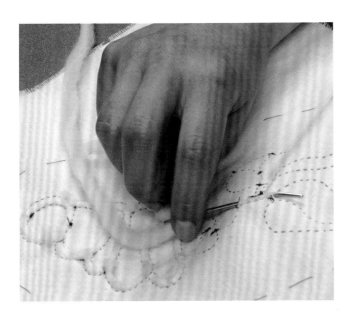

3 To work the corded quilting, use a bodkin or large tapestry needle to run a double thickness of cording wool through the narrow channels. Use the needle to separate threads to start and finish each channel, but do not break through the loose-weave backing except where necessary to turn corners.

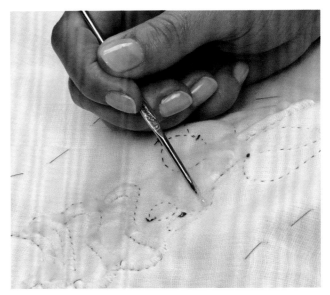

4 To work the stuffed areas, make a hole in the backing and fill the shape with fiberfill or small pieces of batting. Either tease threads back to make an opening large enough to work the stuffing into, or cut a small slit, which will need to be sewn closed when you finish filling the area. We used a fine crochet hook to tease the threads apart and to push stuffing into all the nooks and crannies.

Embroidered Silk Fair Ribbons

Varying the width and number of ribbons in each square will alter the look of this block considerably. The same idea could be worked in strips of fabric, but the fusible web would need to come to the edge of each strip. The joins and seams can be machine-embroidered to cover the raw edges.

MATERIALS FOR ONE BLOCK
⅜ yd (67.5 cm) of thin backing fabric
2 yds (2 m) each of 2 in. (5 cm) wide ribbon in two colors
Lightweight fusible web
Embroidery floss and crewel or embroidery needle

1 Cut 9 in. (22.5 cm) backing squares. We have used four to make a block.

2 Cut 8½ in. (21.5 cm) long strips of 2 in. (5 cm) wide ribbon in two colors. You need four strips per backing square (16 per block).

3 Cut sixteen strips of lightweight fusible web 1 in. (2.5 cm) wide and 8 in. (20 cm) long. Iron one strip to the back side of each strip of ribbon. Center the web lengthwise on the ribbon. Remove the backing paper from each strip. Iron the strips to the backing squares, alternating colors and overlapping the edge of each ribbon very slightly. It is easier to hand embroider the joins if there is no web in the embellished areas, but be careful to keep the overlap even.

4 Embroider the three joins on each square of fused ribbons in your choice of border stitches (see pages 113–114). We have used two strands of cotton floss and worked a mixture of feather stitch, chain stitch, chevron stitch, fly stitch, herringbone stitch, and star stitch.

5 Join the squares, alternating the direction of the strips and the colors of the ribbons. Embroider around the seams to finish the block.

SIGNATURE FANS

One block of this charming fan pattern could be adapted to make a keepsake pillow for a bride or a new mother with members of the wedding party or baby's family signing each fan blade. Enlarge the template (right) to 6 in. (15 cm) along each side.

MATERIALS FOR ONE BLOCK
13 in. (32.5 cm) square of cotton background fabric
6 in. (15 cm) square of contrasting fabric for fan corner
Embroidery floss and crewel or embroidery needle
Sewing thread and appliqué needle
15 in. (37.5 cm) square of batting
Quilting thread and needle

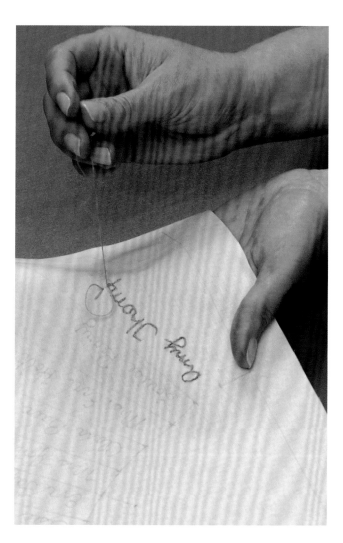

1 Cut a 13 in. (32.5 cm) background square. Use a washout marker to outline the edges of the 11-in. (27.5-cm) square finished block. Enlarge the template of the quarter-circle (above) so each straight side is 6 in. (15 cm) and mark one corner of the block with it. Mark the segments as indicated on the template, then draw the lines to mark the fan "blades."

2 Mark the names or signatures on the blades. Then embroider each name using stem stitch or backstitch. We have used two strands of floss.

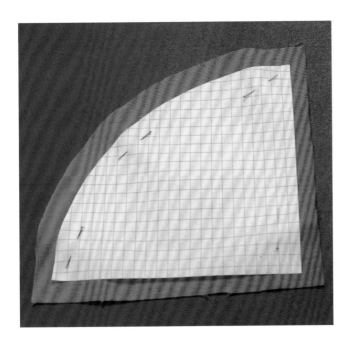

3 Using the quarter-circle template again, make a pattern and cut out the orange quarter-circle piece. Add a generous ¼ in. (6 mm) seam allowance on the curved edge and a generous ½ in. (12 mm) on the straight edges.

4 Pin the quarter-circle in place on the fan block and apply it along the curved edge only.

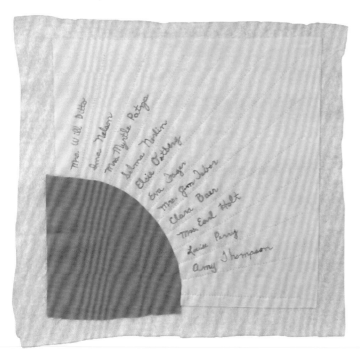

5 Place the block on a 15 in. (37.5 cm) square of batting and hand quilt the lines of the fan blades.

6 Trim the block, leaving a generous ¼ in. (6 mm) seam allowance outside the marked square, and remove the marked lines and written signatures. Then trim the edges to complete the block as an 11 in. (27.5 cm) square.

OLD MAID'S RAMBLE

This lively block is sometimes called London Square. Its seemingly simple construction is deceptive. The lights and darks are arranged differently on adjacent sides, so follow the diagrams carefully. The original uses multicolored scraps for the dark value in the small triangle squares and we have replicated the same idea. It can also be very effective if a limited color palette is used.

MATERIALS FOR ONE BLOCK
White cotton fabric
Mid-blue cotton fabric
Orange cotton fabric
Multicolored scraps of cotton fabric
Rotary cutter, ruler, and mat

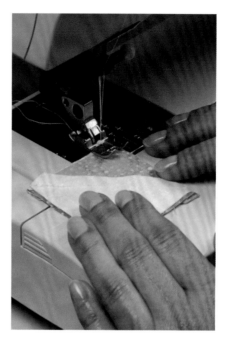

1 Make triangle squares, starting with the orange and white hourglass center. You need two 2¾ in. (7 cm) squares of each color—we have used a strip of each and marked squares on the wrong side of the white in pencil. Mark one diagonal in each square. With right sides together, stitch ¼ in. (6 mm) from the diagonal line along each side. Cut along the diagonal. You will now have four triangle squares. Press each one toward the dark side and trim off the nibs.

2 Join the four triangle squares as shown in the diagram below.

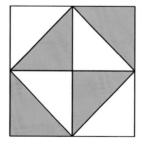

3 Now make the scrap triangle squares. You will need 32 in total. Use a variety of fabrics for the colored side. We used the same white tonal print for the light sides. Join them into four strips of eight triangle squares each, following the diagram below closely. Notice that the arrangement of two of the strips is different from the other two.

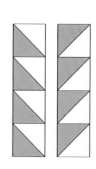

4 Join one strip to each of two opposite sides of the orange and white center, arranging lights and darks as shown in the diagram, below.

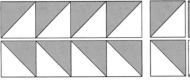
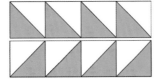

5 Cut one blue and one white 7 in. (17.5 cm) square and cut each one along one diagonal to make two triangles of each color.

6 Add one triangle of each color to each of the remaining two scrap-triangle strips. Pay attention to the arrangement of the lights and darks, following the diagram, below, carefully.

7 Join the two large pieced triangles to the sides of the pieced strip.

8 Cut four white and four scrap 2¾ in. (7 cm) triangles. Join in light and dark pairs. Note that two are mirror images of the others.

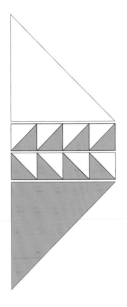

9 Add one of the resulting pieced triangles to each corner of the block as shown. Press.

WREATH AND DOVE STEPS

This charming doll's quilt pattern could also be used to make a folk art pillow, or it could become the centerpiece of a larger appliqué quilt. The templates can be found on pages 135).

MATERIALS FOR ONE BLOCK
17 in. (42.5 cm) square of cotton background fabric
Scraps of red and green cotton fabric
17 in. (42.5 cm) square of 4-gauge clear vinyl film
Freezer paper
Ultrafine permanent marker pen
Washable white marker pencil
Appliqué pins
Sewing thread and appliqué needle
Cotton embroidery floss and embroidery needle

1 Cut a 17 in. (42.5 cm) background square. Fold it in half twice to find the center point. Cut a 17 in. (42.5 cm) square of 4-gauge clear vinyl film and use an ultrafine permanent marker to mark the center with a small dot. Mark the center of each side with registration marks that can be matched to the fabric square.

2 Using the permanent marker, enlarge and trace the full template on page 135 onto the vinyl film. Trace the individual templates onto the paper side of freezer paper and cut out. The number of each shape needed is indicated on the template. Cut four strips of freezer paper ½ x 14 in. (12 mm x 35 cm).

3 Iron the freezer paper shapes to the right side of the appropriate fabrics. Cut 1 x 15 in. (2.5 x 37.5 cm) bias strips from the green fabric and iron the freezer paper strips to them. Cut out, leaving a seam allowance. Press lightly with an iron but be careful not to pull the bias edges out of shape as you work.

4 Trace around each shape with a fine-point removable marker and cut out each shape, leaving a generous ¼ in.. (6 mm) seam allowance. Fingerpress the seam allowance to the wrong side all around each shape.

5 Line up the background square and the vinyl pattern and position the bird shape.

6 Use small appliqué pins to anchor the bird in place, pinning inside the marked line. Turn the seam allowance under along the marked line as you apply the bird piece to the background using thread to match the color of the bird. Use small appliqué stitches that do not show on the right side of the piece.

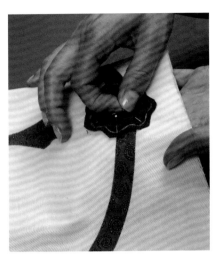

7 Use the vinyl pattern again to position the pieces in order. Add the green shapes surrounding the bird, turning the ends under and butting them up against the red fabric of the bird.

8 Use the vinyl pattern to position the corner buds and sew them in place. There is no need to turn under the stem end of each green portion, as they will be covered by the bias-strip wreath. Then add the green bias strips in four sections to make the wreath. Make sure the curve is smooth and the width of the strips is even.

9 Cover each join between the wreath sections with a red flower. Pinning as shown here makes it easy to work and also to remove the pins as you finish each section.

10 Working the same way, add the leaves.

11 Satin stitch the center of each flower using a strand of yellow floss. Make the bird's eye in the same way using a darker shade of floss. Press the entire block from the wrong side to remove the fold.

FLORAL QUILTS
Trees and Flowers, *page 24*

This quilt is made up of four large blocks, each 30 in. (75 cm) square. The background fabric is white cotton with an appliqué design of a green tree with leaves

and red berries and two red birds sitting at the base of each tree. The brown grapevine border, with its green leaves and brown grapes, and the central yellow and red flower or sun and flying red and yellow birds were probably added once the four large blocks were fully completed and sewn together. The border is made of wide strips of plain cotton fabric that have been added to the top and bottom. The finished quilt has batting and backing and has been quilted along all four sides with simple horizontal lines.

Techniques needed for this quilt:
Appliqué, page 113
Adding a border, page 115
Batting and backing, page 115

FLORAL QUILTS
Nosegay, *Page 26*

Each Nosegay block is made up of one

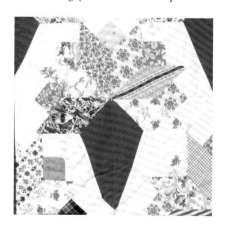

blue kite-shape, six triangles in a selection of fabrics fanning around at the top and five smaller triangles inset, all pieced on a white background. The 54 blocks are set on point and with a 3½-inch (9-cm) wide plain blue border. The finished quilt has batting and backing, and is tied at intervals.

Techniques needed for this quilt:
Joining fabric pieces, page 113
Adding a border, page 115
Batting and backing, page 115
Tying, page 115

FLORAL QUILTS
President's Wreath, *Page 28*

The 12 blocks that make up this quilt are each 17 in. (42.5 cm) square. Each block has a plain white muslin background with an appliqué of four red flowers with yellow

centers set over a circular green ring, with green leaves at intervals. Green bell-shaped flowers are arranged at intervals on both sides of the ring, one inside and two outside, each with a red "stamen." White muslin has been used for the sashing and borders, which are both 5 in. (12.5 cm) wide. The backing fabric is a blue and white polka dot, which is turned to the front to make a simple quarter-inch (6 mm) binding. The finished quilt has batting and backing, and is quilted with diagonal lines of hand-stitching over the entire background, running from edge to edge in one direction.

Techniques needed for this quilt:
Appliqué, page 113
Adding sashing, page 114
Adding a border, page 115
Batting and backing, page 115
Binding, page 115

WHOLECLOTH QUILTS
Pink Calamanco Wholecloth, *Page 38*

The top of this quilt is pieced from four strips each approximately 24 in. (60 cm) wide. The quilting patterns are traditional, with a typical central area that includes a floral design and a heart-shaped motif

surrounded by an elaborate running feather pattern that dips in and out in a roughly rectangular shape. Each of the four corners has a pointed oval motif, joined by a running feather border that echoes the center one. Floral designs appear at intervals around the border, some part of the border feather pattern, others freestanding. Fine diagonal lines approximately a quarter-inch (6 mm) apart fill every area of the background outside the motifs. The batting and backing are both wool, with the backing pieced from a green and white homespun check about 10 in. (25 cm) wide along the sides, with a central panel of brown linsey-woolsey. The the front and back edges of the quilt have been turned to the middle and stitched in place to make the binding.

Techniques needed for this quilt:
Joining fabric pieces, page 113
Batting and backing, page 115
Binding, page 115

WHOLECLOTH QUILTS
Children's Comforter,
Page 40

The top and backing of this quilt are both pieced from large pieces of printed cotton fabric that are likely to have originated as

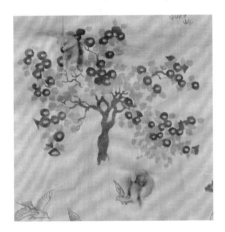

feedsacks. The quilt is held together with randomly spaced ties in turquoise cotton thread; a number of the ties have been placed in the center of some of the red balloons the girl is holding. The edge-to-middle binding has been stitched by machine.

Techniques needed for this quilt:
Joining fabric pieces, page 113
Batting and backing, page 115
Binding, 115
Tying, page 115

EMBELLISHED QUILTS
Redwork Quilt, *Page 50*

The top of this quilt is made up of 30 blocks, each with a motif embroidered in backstitch or stem stitch on plain white cotton using red embroidery floss. The motifs were probably pre-printed squares, or embroidery transfers may have been

used. The blocks are joined edge to edge and quilted with a simple crosshatch grid. The plain outside border has a quilted triple cable pattern.

Techniques needed for this quilt:
Embroidery, page 113–114
Joining fabric pieces, page 113
Adding a border, page 115
Batting and backing, page 115

EMBELLISHED QUILTS
Crazy Quilt with Fans,
Page 52

This quilt is made up of fifty crazy foundation squares combined to make a full quilt, a method known as contained crazy or crazy block pattern. Scraps of

fabric are laid on the foundation square and basted in place, then the raw edges are turned under and covered with decorative embroidery stitches worked through the backing. An alternative method is to sew pieces to the foundation square using the stitch-and-flip technique and then embellish the seams with fancy stitches. The squares have been set on point and smaller square blocks, sometimes made from only two fabrics, have been used to fill in the edges, creating a chevron design that is bound in beige silk. Most of the

larger squares contain at least one embroidered scrap, and some fabrics have a date written on them. The embroidery on crazy quilts is either done before the blocks are joined or at the same time as the decorative seaming is worked.

Techniques needed for this quilt:
Piecing a foundation block, page 113
Embroidery, pages 113–114
Batting and backing, page 115
Binding, page 115

EMBELLISHED QUILTS
Embroidered Wool Lap Quilt, *Page 54*

The thirty-six rectangular patches in this lap quilt are each 5 x 8 in. (12.5 x 20 cm), and probably began life as samples in book of wool suiting fabrics. Each patch has a delicate and colorful embroidered flower and the seams between the patches are decorated with multicolored feather stitching. The embroidery is worked in wool yarn and pearl cotton. The backing is wool plaid, a teal, navy, black, red, and yellow twill. The quilt is tied with navy-blue thread, with the ties on the back. The binding is edges to middle.

Techniques needed for this quilt:
Joining fabric pieces, page 113
Embroidery, pages 113–114
Batting and backing, page 115
Binding, page 115
Tying, page 115

SIGNATURE QUILTS
Chimney Sweep, *Page 64*

The 36 blocks on this quilt are pieced with a pattern of colored squares surrounding a pale-colored central cross, which can be made from five light-colored squares, or two squares and a rectangle of the same

width and three times the length of the squares. Setting the blocks on point makes the signed strips appear horizontal; the names are written in ink. The quilting is a simple cable on the sashing strips, while a series of squares quilted parallel to the edges of each block run counter to the seams to hold the batting securely in place.

Techniques needed for this quilt:
Piecing shapes, page 115
Adding a border, page 115
Batting and backing, page 115

SIGNATURE QUILTS
Red and White Chevron, *Page 66*

This quilt is pieced from interlocking rectangles and squares offset to create a highly unusual chevron or zigzag design. It carries the signatures of 455 people, each of which has been written in ink on a

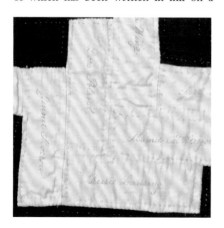

white strip, and the central red area is embroidered in white with an inscription in a tight stem stitch. Each separate rectangle is outline quilted on the inside of the shape. The backing is muslin, and all of the edges are finished with a narrow red binding.

Techniques needed for this quilt:
Piecing shapes, page 113
Adding sashing, page 114
Binding, page 115
Batting and backing, page 115

SIGNATURE QUILTS
Oak Leaf, *Page 68*

Each of the 49 blocks on this quilt is 12 in. (30 cm) square. Each block has four appliquéd oak leaves of print fabric, with opposites matching each other in each block. The leaves spring from a small

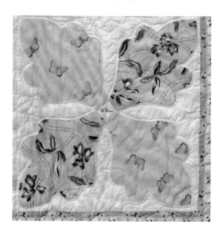

central square, and these squares contain the ink-lettered signatures, most decorated with a tiny drawing although some are blurred. The background is white cotton and the mitered border, around three sides, is printed with a gold, white, and green floral vine climbing a trellis. The leaves are outline quilted.

Techniques needed for this quilt:
Appliqué, page 113
Joining fabric pieces, page 113
Adding a border, page 115
Batting and backing, page 115

GEOMETRIC QUILTS
Chinese Coins, *Page 78*

This quilt is pieced in a design that was popular in the Amish tradition called Chinese Coins, or Roman Coins, or Roman Stripe. It is constructed from strips

of silk and velvet dressmaking scraps sewn together into seven 7-inch (17.5-cm) wide bands that are alternated and bordered with narrow dark blue velvet strips. The backing

is a striped silk taffeta in purple and gray with a bias border mitered at the corners.

Techniques needed for this quilt:
Joining fabric pieces, page 113
Adding sashing, page 114
Adding a border, page 115
Batting and backing, page 115

GEOMETRIC QUILTS
Modern Blocks, *Page 80*

It is constructed from 72 dark-toned blocks and 56 light-toned blocks, plus 23 half blocks to straighten the edges. Each block is made of five strips of equal width and most contain three different fabrics— all silk and velvet dressmaking scraps—

arranged to balance within the block but to give an overall impression of the block being light or dark. The blocks are set on point to create alternating vertical rows of light and dark, and the strips alternate with darks pointing in one direction and the lights running the other way. The inner border is made of black velvet in an unusual octagonal shape, its edges embroidered with a floral garland on the inside and a double zigzag with long stitches, similar to a tuft of grass or an ear of wheat, on the outer side. The outer border is pieced from narrow alternating triangles scalloped on the outside similar to an ice cream cone. The scallops are embroidered with tight buttonhole stitch.

Techniques needed for this quilt:
Piecing shapes, page 113
Adding a border, page 115
Embroidery, pages 113–114
Batting and backing, page 115

GEOMETRIC QUILTS
Courthouse Steps, *Page 82*

This quilt has 72 blocks in a design called Courthouse Steps, which has light and dark strips of multicolored cotton stitched on opposite sides of a central red square, thought to represent the fire or hearth at

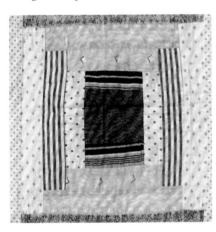

the heart of every home. The blocks are joined in rows without sashing. The batting is cotton, the backing plain muslin, and the quilt is bound with a cotton print.

Techniques needed for this quilt:
Piecing strips, page 113
Batting and backing, page 115
Binding, page 115

GEOMETRIC QUILTS –
Honeycomb Quilt, *Page 84*

The traditional method for stitching hexagons, only two sides of which can ever be on the straight of grain, is the English paper piecing method. Paper templates are cut to the finished size; then fabric pieces are cut slightly larger and basted to the paper template. The shapes are joined with

whipstitch or buttonhole stitch and then the papers are removed so the quilt can be layered and quilted. In this quilt six hexagons in bright fabrics are joined in a

ring around a seventh to make a rosette that is outlined with a background row of white muslin. A similar fabric has been used for the 3-inch (7.5-cm) wide borders and for the backing. It is simply quilted in parallel lines and filled with wool batting.

Techniques needed for this quilt:
English paper piecing, page 113
Adding a border, page 115
Batting and backing, page 115

CRIB QUILTS
Irish Chain, *Page 92*

This Triple Irish Chain design is made from 1½-inch (4 cm) red and white cotton squares. The chain and the four white triangular areas in the center of each side of the X are all set square, while the outside edges are made as a pieced border

using squares of red set on point and separated by white triangles on either side. The quilt is tied in different ways: the white squares, and the four red corner squares, with quarter-inch-wide (6 mm) red silk

ribbons, each about 6 inches (15 cm) long. The red squares have white cotton embroidery floss ties. The backing is white muslin, and the back-to-front binding is held in place with feather stitch worked with pink embroidery floss, with the same floss used to tie the red border squares.

Techniques needed for this quilt:
Piecing shapes, page 113
Batting and backing, page 115
Binding, page 115
Embroidery, pages 113–114
Tying, page 115

CRIB QUILTS
Flying Geese Crib Quilt, *Page 94*

This quilt is made up of 100 Flying Geese blocks set in parallel rows pointing in the same direction and divided by long unpieced strips. Each block is made from one large right-angle triangle with two smaller right-angle triangles arranged one

on each short side of the large triangle to create a rectangle. The colored cotton fabric used for the larger triangles has narrow stripes of green, yellow, and blue, with green as the dominant color, and the smaller triangles and alternate strips are white cotton. The same white cotton has been used for the backing, while a narrow binding of double brown printed cotton fabric finishes the edges. The quilting, which covers the entire quilt, is simple diagonal crosshatching.

Techniques needed for this quilt:
Piecing shapes, page 113
Joining fabric pieces, page 113
Batting and backing, page 115
Binding, page 115

CRIB QUILTS
Sunburst Crib Quilt, *Page 96*

The Sunburst design is composed entirely of 60-degree diamonds sewn together to create an explosion of color. It is traditionally been constructed using the English paper piecing method, as described

in the Honeycomb Quilt on page 131. This example begins with an eight-pointed star in a narrow red-and-white stripe and continues in rings of contrasting color all the way to the edges of the quilt. The first ring is a pale blue solid fabric with points in pale yellow. The next ring is darker in value and composed from a dark red and a dark blue print with beige points. The following rings alternate in value, with the fabrics in carefully balanced pairs, and the outer points of each ring different from the other fabrics in that ring. The backing is brown and blue check, while the binding is a blue and white floral print. The quilting follows the shapes of the diamond pieces.

Techniques needed for this quilt:
English paper piecing, page 113
Batting and backing, page 115
Binding, page 115

CRIB QUILTS
Brick Wall, *Page 100*

The Brick Wall pattern is made of rectangles stitched into long strips end to end, and then joining the strips in rows. The rectangles are offset row by row to make the piece look like a real wall

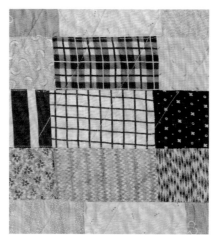

constructed from building bricks. The fabrics used in this quilt include calico prints and woven geometric patterns, both checks and stripes. The predominant color is red, with a scattering of browns, pinks, beiges, and blues, including one small patch of dark blue in contrast with the pale blues found elsewhere. The backing is a red and white striped cotton that has also been used to make the binding. The entire quilt is machine pieced, and the machine quilting is worked in diagonal lines.

Techniques needed for this quilt:
Piecing shapes, page 113
Batting and backing, page 115
Binding, page 115

CRIB QUILTS
Texas Star Crib Quilt, *Page 102*

Texas Star is a variation of an eight-point star and it is easy to create, since the points are all right-angle triangles in a nine-patch formation. The twelve pieced star blocks are made from solid-colored and patterned cotton fabrics, some printed and some woven in geometric patterns, either checks or stripes. They are set on point and separated with setting squares and triangles made from a brown and green striped taffeta fabric. The unfinished edges are not

bound, and the piece is not quilted, but has a white cotton backing.

Techniques needed for this quilt:
Piecing shapes, page 113
Batting and backing, page 115

DOLL QUILTS
Nine-Patch Quilt, *Page 104*

This quilt is made of twelve nine-patch blocks made with multicolored fabric scraps, set with sashing between each block. The sashing is brown and blue, the binding a red check. The backing is a coarse brown and white check, there is no batting and the piece is not quilted.

Techniques needed for this quilt:
Joining fabric pieces, page 113
Sashing, page 114
Backing, page 115
Binding, page 115

Cotton Reel Quilt, *Page 105*

The Cotton Reel, or Hourglass, quilt has twelve quarter-square triangle blocks made of a varied selection of men's tie silk. There

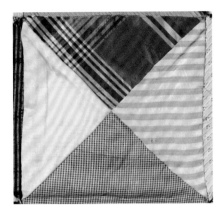

are stripes, solids, checks, and woven patterns in an alternating light and dark configuration. The backing is polished cotton, and it is bound edges to middle. There is no quilting.

Techniques needed for this quilt:
Piecing shapes, page 113
Batting and backing, page 115
Binding, page 115

Four-Patch Quilt, *Page 106*

This quilt is made of twelve four-patch blocks made with multicolored fabric scraps, set with sashing between each

block. Each block has either brown or beige patches, and the sashing is a roller-printed geometric. The backing is also

brown, and brown tones predominate in the paisley binding.

Techniques needed for this quilt:
Joining fabric pieces, page 113
Adding sashing. page 114
Batting and backing, page 115
Binding, page 115

One-Patch Quilt, *Page 107*

This one-patch quilt has a central nine-patch block creating a cross in the middle. The printed cotton fabrics are brightly colored and the squares alternate between lights and darker shades; browns

predominate, but there are also pinks, blues, red, and green check. Backing and binding are the same brown-and-white floral print. The quilt is machine quilted in vertical rows through the center of the squares with two horizontal rows, one in the center and one through the bottom row.

Techniques needed for this quilt:
Joining fabric pieces, page 113
Borders, page 115
Batting and backing, page 115
Binding, page 115

One-Patch Quilt, *Page 108*

The one-patch quilt on page 108 is made of 66 squares of dress silks. The back is also silk, pieced from three different fabrics. Two of the fabrics used on the back have also been used to make the side borders,

which are pieced from two one-inch strips on one side and a simple two-inch border on the other. The binding on this quilt is edges to middle.

Techniques needed for this quilt:
Joining fabric pieces, page 113
Batting and backing, page 115
Binding, page 115

Four-Patch Quilt, *Page 109*

The final quilt is a simple four-patch, with the blocks set edge to edge. The printed cottons are primarily pinks and browns,

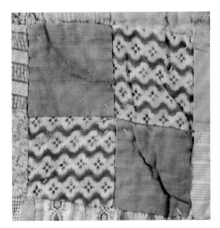

with blues, greens, and one yellow. Batted in cotton and backed in cream muslin, the piece is quilted in a crosshatch along the diagonal of each patch. The edge is bound in plain cream.

Techniques needed for this quilt:
Joining fabric pieces, page 113
Batting and backing, page 115
Binding, page 115

TEMPLATES

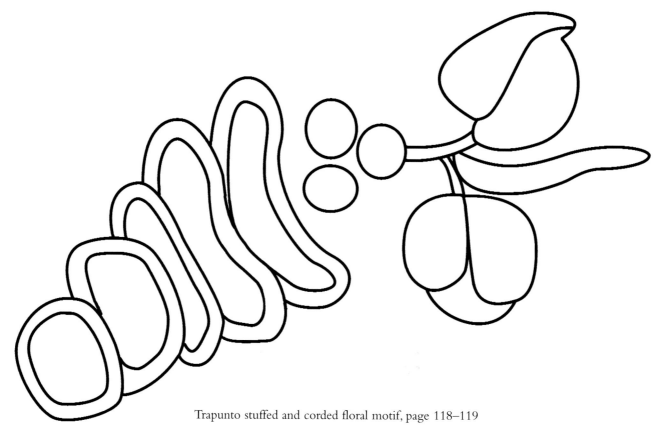

Trapunto stuffed and corded floral motif, page 118–119

Alternative Trapunto stuffed leaf motif quilt template

Alternative Trapunto stuffed and corded floral motif quilt template

Alternative Trapunto Quilt template

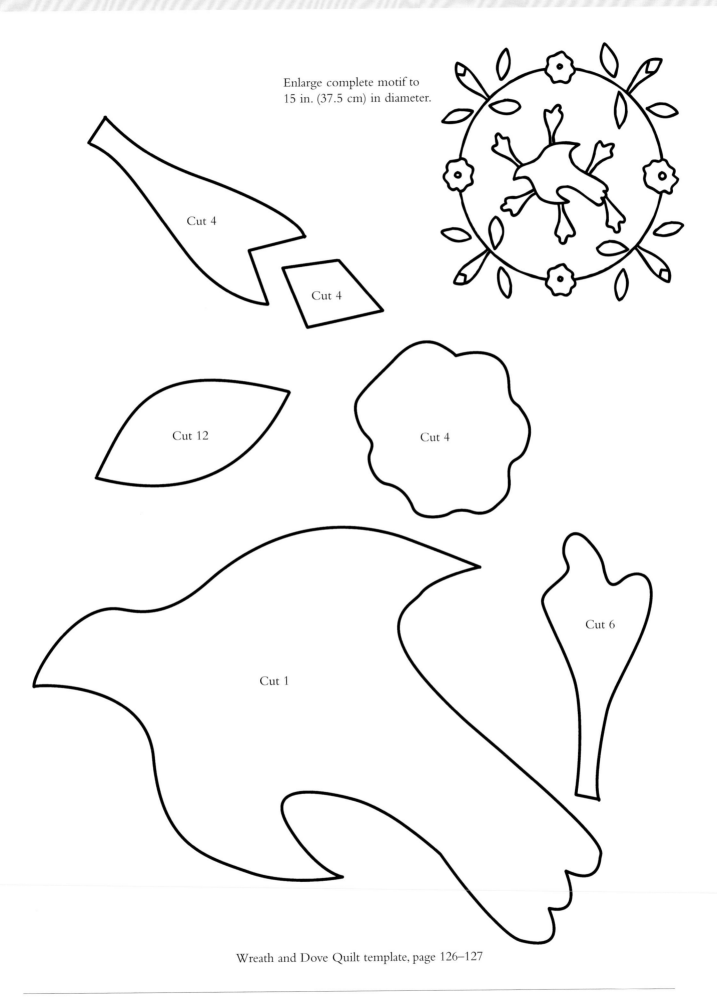

Enlarge complete motif to
15 in. (37.5 cm) in diameter.

Cut 4

Cut 4

Cut 12

Cut 4

Cut 1

Cut 6

Wreath and Dove Quilt template, page 126–127

GLOSSARY

appliqué
The process of applying small pieces of fabric to a larger piece of background cloth.

backing
The third, bottom, or back layer of a quilt sandwich

Baltimore Album
A distinctive style of appliqué used to make quilts, which originated in Baltimore, Maryland, in the 1840s. Bright-colored motifs showing plants and animals, buildings, patriotic designs, baskets and vases, and even people abound.

basting
The process of joining two or more layers of fabric temporarily to hold them in place while final stitching is done. Basting can be done with safety pins or needle and thread.

batting
Fiber filling used as the middle layer of a quilt. It can be made from polyester, a poly-cotton blend, cotton, silk, or wool, and provides the warmth expected of a quilt. Also called a batt. Today's commercial batting is processed to stabilize the fibers. In the past quilts were batted with loose fibers of wool or cotton, old blankets, and even older, worn-out quilts.

bias
The diagonal grain of a woven fabric between the lengthwise and crosswise grains. True bias is cut at a 45- degree angle to the straight of grain. Any bias-cut fabric stretches easily but is less subject to fraying than straight-cut cloth.

borders
Strips of fabric added to the edges of a quilt top to enclose and frame it. They can be wide or narrow and pieced or plain.

broderie perse
An appliqué technique in which printed motifs from one fabric are cut out and applied to a different background cloth, both to stretch the life of the design cloth and to create new patterns.

calamanco
A woolen fabric polished or glazed by being subjected to heat and pressure. Its strength and luster made it particularly popular for wholecloth quilts during the colonial era in North America.

corded quilting
Also known as Italian quilting. A type of quilting in which a narrow channel is stitched through two layers of fabric and a cord or yarn is inserted between the layers to create a raised design area.

cotton
A natural fiber from the cotton plant that can be woven into cloth or spun into thread in a variety of weights and thicknesses. It is ideal for quiltmaking. *See also Batting*

coverlet
A bedcover. Coverlets can be woven, but many are made from quilt tops with backing, but with no batting or quilting.

crazy quilt
A type of quilt particularly popular in the Victorian era of the latter half of the nineteenth century in which small randomly shaped pieces of fabric, generally dressmaking scraps and often luxurious, are applied to a foundation and embellished with embroidery, inked drawings or text.

cross-grain
Also known as crosswise grain or width. The cross grain of a woven fabric is perpendicular to the selvages. It has more stretch than is found in the lengthwise threads.

embellishment
Decoration applied to a quilt top, mainly in the form of embroidery.

embroidery
The process of decorating fabric by hand or machine by stitching designs onto the surface of the cloth using thread or yarn.

embroidery floss
A popular embroidery thread, usually made from cotton but also found in rayon or silk, which is stranded. Cotton floss has six strands,

and lengths can be divided and used individually or in combinations of two, three, or more, depending on the desired effect.

four-patch
A type of quilt block in which four squares of the same size and different fabrics are combined. Each square can be plain or pieced to make a more intricate pattern.

frame
A square or rectangular shape created with four sticks of wood or plastic tubing for mounting the layers of a quilt to hold them taut for quilting.

frameless quilting
Working without a frame to quilt, usually when working a small piece or a single block.

geometric patterns
Patterns based on geometric shapes, which are the basis for most patchwork blocks.

handwork
Stitching done by hand as opposed to machine sewn.

heirloom
An item of intrinsic or personal value that is, or can be, handed down from one generation to another.

hoop
A round frame consisting of two concentric circles that fit inside each other. The size of the large, outside circle can be adjusted with a screw. A hoop can be used to hold handwork such as quilting or embroidery.

kit quilt
A type of quilt that has the pattern, directions, and fabric all included in one package. Kit quilts were particularly popular in the first half of the twentieth century.

lightbox
A tool consisting of a transparent or translucent table with a built-in light source used to trace a design or pattern through a dark layer of fabric or paper.

linen
A natural fiber from the flax plant that can be processed into a firm thread that can be used for sewing or woven into cloth.

marker
Any pen or pencil that can be used to mark fabric. They can be permanent or removable, and should always be tested on the fabric before being used.

masking tape
A type of low-tack tape that can be easily removed from fabric or hard surfaces. Found in the equipment of most quiltmakers.

needles
Thin metal shaft used for sewing by hand or machine. Needles are pointed or rounded at one end and have a slit called an eye at the other through which a length of thread is inserted. Machine needles have a thicker shaft at one end, with the eye just above the pointed tip. There are many types, all designed to make a particular sewing task efficient and comfortable. There are special needles for quilting (betweens), embroidery (crewel, tapestry), sewing (sharps), beading and millinery work, and machine work. All types are available in several sizes.

nine-patch
A type of quilt block in which nine units, usually of the same size and generally but not always square, are combined. Each unit can be plain or pieced to make a more intricate design.

one-patch
A type of quilt pattern in which one shape is used throughout. These can be triangular, square, rectangular, diamond, or hexagonal.

patchwork
See piecing.

pens
Marking tools that make their marks using ink. There are numerous specialized types available, including washout, fadeout, and permanent versions.

pencil
Marking tools that make their marks using leads, such as graphite, watercolor, and mechanical versions.

piecing
A process of sewing fabrics together by hand or machine to create a larger piece of cloth. Also referred to as patchwork.

pin
Implement usually made of metal used to hold fabric layers together or attach patterns to fabric temporarily. Straight pins have a sharp point at one end and a small flat head at the other to hold the pin in place. Safety pins are shaped and have a catch that holds them closed. Pins come in many sizes and several thicknesses, including short appliqué pins, long, large-headed quilt pins, and very fine silk pins.

pincushion
A small cushion or magnetic device for holding pins ready for use.

plaid
A type of fabric with stripes of different colors and widths that cross each other in both directions at right angles. Plaid, also called tartan, can be woven or printed.

polyester
A type of synthetic fiber widely used for making cloth. Polyester can be blended with cotton, and both 100% polyester and cotton/poly blends are generally less expensive than pure cotton. It is less supple than cotton cloth.

printed fabric
Any woven fabric with a design that has been stamped onto the fabric.

quilt
An item, usually a bedcover, made from two layers of fabric with a layer of filling, such as batting, in between. The fabric layers can be single pieces, or they can be pieced. In the case of appliqué quilts, usually only the top surface is worked with applied designs.

quilting
The stitching that holds the layers of a quilt together permanently. The stitch is usually a type of running stitch.

redwork
A type of quilt popular in the early twentieth century made from embroidered squares or panels joined together to make a bedcover. Motifs are usually realistic though childlike, and most examples were worked on white or cream background fabrics in red embroidery floss, hence the name.

sampler quilt
A type of quilt in which each block is different.

sashing
Strips of fabric used to separate blocks in a quilt.

sawtooth
A zigzag design found in many quilt patterns.

scissors
A cutting tool consisting of two blades joined at the fulcrum by a screw. There are many sizes and types available, each designed for specific uses, including fabric scissors (which should only be used to cut cloth), pinking shears (which have a zigzag, or "pinked" edge that helps to stop fraying), general scissors for cutting paper, batting, etc., embroidery scissors (which are small and sharp), and thread snips, to name a few.

seam allowance
The gap between the raw edge and the seam line of a piece of fabric, which is generally turned under so that it is not seen on top of the work. In patchwork and appliqué, the seam allowance is usually ¼ in. (6 mm) or less.

sets
The way the elements in a quilt are combined, or "set".

setting squares and triangles
Shapes used to square off a quilt top, especially when the blocks are set diagonally, or "on point."

silk
A natural fiber from the cocoon of the silkworm. It is considered the finest thread from which to make cloth, but it can be tricky to handle as it is slippery and frays easily.

stab stitch
A stitch used in quilting and embroidery in which the needle and thread are taken through the layers of fabric perpendicular and in only one direction at a time.

stem stitch
An outline embroidery stitch widely used in redwork.

stencil
A type of template used to mark quilting patterns onto a quilt top. The design is cut out of a piece of plastic or cardboard, and marking is done by drawing through the openings in the stencil.

straight of grain
The straight, up-and-down direction of the threads in a woven fabric. Lengthwise threads (the warp) run parallel to the selvage and create the most stable direction; threads that run across the width (the weft), or cross grain, are perpendicular to the selvage and have a bit more elasticity. *See also bias.*

strip piecing
Combining strips of fabric that are then cut into units and reconfigured to create block patterns.

strippy quilt
A type of quilt widely made in the second half of the nineteenth century consisting of vertical strips of alternating fabrics. Strippies were usually quilted with a separate design for each strip.

template
A shaped piece of firm but flexible material such as plastic, cardboard, or heavy paper used as a pattern for marking an appliqué, piecing or quilting design on fabric. They can be purchased or made by hand with seam allowances optional.

thimble
A tool designed to shield the finger or thumb from being pricked by the needle while stitching by hand. Thimbles come in numerous shapes and sizes, and can be made from metal, plastic, leather, or even rubber.

thread
A twisted strand of fiber that has been spun into a continuous filament. Almost any fiber can be used, but quiltmakers generally work with thread made from cotton, polyester, silk, or nylon, which is used to make a clear version known as invisible thread.

trapunto
A type of quilting in which parts of the quilting pattern are stuffed from the back to create raised areas on the surface of the quilt. Elements in motifs are emphasized by making them three-dimensional by stuffing them from the back or running a cord or yarn through stitched channels.

turkey red
A type of red fabric that was hugely popular for making quilts in the latter half of the nineteenth century. It was dyed with the first colorfast red dye.

wadding
See batting.

wholecloth
A type of quilt that appears to have been made from one piece of fabric.

wool
A natural fiber made from the coats of sheep and some other wooly animals such as alpaca. It is warm and moisture resistant, and can be spun into yarn or woven into fabric in a variety of weights.

woven fabric
Fabric in which the pattern is formed by weaving pre-dyed threads of various colors into patterns, such as plaids or checks and motifs. *See also printed fabric.*

WISCONSIN HISTORICAL SOCIETY

The Wisconsin Historical Society.

This book could not have happened without the enthusiastic cooperation and wholehearted support of the Wisconsin Historical Society, and I thank everyone who contributed time, energy, and ideas to the effort.

The Wisconsin Historical Society is based in Madison, the beautiful lake-rich capital of Wisconsin, which is also home to the University of Wisconsin. Founded in 1846, two years before statehood, the Society is both a state agency and a private membership organization. Chartered in 1853, the Society is the longest serving, publicly supported historical society in the nation. It is charged by statute with collecting, advancing, and disseminating knowledge of Wisconsin and North American history. It began life in the south wing of the State Capitol building, located on a hilltop in Madison's Capitol Square, but by the mid-1890s its quarters had become crowded, and its director, Reuben Gold Thwaites, began planning for a move to a building dedicated to the Society and its mission. Because university students used the library in far greater numbers than any other group, Thwaites enlisted the support of Charles Kendall Adams, president of the university, to establish a base on the university campus. Together they lobbied and eventually won the support of the state Legislature to build a new facility, which opened on October 19, 1900, before an audience of 900 invited guests. Today the Society serves more than 2 million people annually in pursuing its ongoing mission of helping people connect with the past.

Opposite the Capitol building on a corner of Capitol Square stands the Wisconsin Historical Museum, with collections of 110,000 historical objects and nearly 350,000 archaeological artifacts. The museum offers permanent and online exhibitions as well as an ongoing series of changing exhibits.

Old World Wisconsin, where the pictures of quilts that open each chapter of the book were photographed, is one of ten historic sites around the state owned by the Society. Established near the small town of Eagle in 1976 as a Wisconsin contribution to the American bicentennial, Old World Wisconsin re-creates the life of early settlers to the state. Historic structures from around the state have been moved to the 576-acre site to create groups of buildings that honor the various ethnic groups that accepted the challenges of life on the frontier from the 1840s into the early 1900s. It is above all a living history museum, with working farms and livestock, village buildings where business and community socialization were conducted, and the homes of village residents. Costumed interpreters carry out the tasks that comprised the daily routine of pioneers and explain to visitors how life was lived on the frontier.

I would like to thank the Wisconsin Historical Society from the bottom of my heart for its help and enthusiasm in making this book happen.

INDEX

ACKNOWLEDGMENTS

This book would not have been possible without the full cooperation and support of the Wisconsin Historical Society of Madison, Wisconsin. In particular I would like to thank Leslie Bellais, curator of textiles, who took the idea and ran with it straight to Ann Koski, director of the Wisconsin Historical Museum, who got the Society on board. The two, with their colleague at Old World Wisconsin, Ellen Penwell, made sure that everything needed was taken care of in time to meet a tight deadline. Thanks to them all.

And to Colin Gower, who made sure the project went ahead and has been supportive throughout. Marie Clayton has worked her usual magic to edit and contribute her own thoughts and ideas to my text. Sue Rose has chosen, from the myriad photographs available, the best, and designed a lively and beautiful book. Mark Hines spent many hours lighting, photographing, and downloading the wonderful pictures. Michelle Hines was the perfect hand model.

Thanks also to Patricia Thompson who created the materials for the Fan Quilt step-by-step photographs and the triangle squares for the Baskets quilt project, and to Susan Popp, who made the charming Wreath and Dove doll quilt and its associated steps. Both made sure their samples for the projects were ready on time and beautifully worked.

And as always, to David, who encourages my ideas and efforts, and gives me the space to carry them out.